Young Adult Faith-Launchers

Loveland, Colorado

Young Adult Faith-Launchers

Copyright © 1998 Group Publishing, Inc.

Credits

Editor: Debbie Gowensmith
Creative Development Editor: Paul Woods
Chief Creative Officer: Joani Schultz
Copy Editor: Helen Turnbull
Art Director: Ray Tollison
Cover Art Director: Jeff A. Storm
Computer Graphic Artist: Books International
Production Manager: Gingar Kunkel

Library of Congress Cataloging-in-Publication Data
Young adult faith-launchers.
        p. cm.
    Includes index.
    ISBN 0-7644-2037-2 (alk. paper)
    1. Church work with young adults. 2. Bible—Study and teaching.
  3. Young adults—Religous life.
  BV4446.Y68   1997
  268'.434—dc21   97-37780
                                                                                  CIP

10 9 8 7 6 5 4 3 2   07 06 05 04 03 02 01 00 99 98

Printed in the United States of America.

▼Table of Contents

▼Contributors

Many thanks to these writers of Group's Real Life Bible Curriculum and Core Belief Bible Study Series, whose creative ideas and expertise constitute this book:

▶

Bob Buller	Karl Leuthauser
Beth Copeland	Mike Nappa
John Cutshall	Helen Turnbull
Debbie Harned	Jane Vogel
Mikal Keefer	Michael D. Warden
Lisa Baba Lauffer	Paul Woods
Rick Lawrence	

▼Introduction

OK, you've got these...er...kids to teach. Well, not kids really, but not mature adults either. Some are in college or graduate school, some are already in jobs and careers, some are still living with parents, some are living on their own. Not kids, but barely adults. Young adults.

Young adults—eighteen- to twenty-five-year-olds—are experiencing their fullest independence to date. They're exposed to new ideas and concepts, and they need more than their parents' opinions, beliefs, or faith to fall back on. They're creating their own.

So what do you want to teach them?

This is where *Young Adult Faith-Launchers* comes in. With eighteen lessons that help students nurture their new, independent faith, you can choose the topics that best fit your group. You can review the fundamentals, such as who Jesus is and why the Bible is relevant to life. You can explore hot topics, such as cults and the New Age movement. And you can examine issues of special interest to this age group, such as busyness and love.

All the studies are presented in fresh, creative, and fun ways that get young adults actively participating, interacting with others, and learning. The end result? Young adults with a deeper faith and new relationships to carry them to adulthood.

What do the studies include?

Young Adult Faith-Launchers is divided into three sections of six lessons. "Looking Up" focuses on fundamentals of the Christian faith, such as Jesus, God, and the Holy Spirit. "Looking In" focuses on personal faith issues, such as priorities and spiritual growth. "Looking Out" focuses on applying faith toward outside issues, such as suffering and families.

Each study concentrates on a **biblical point**—for example, "Faith in Jesus is the only way to eternal life." This is the heart of the study, the message each person should leave with.

The point reflects a message found in Scripture; this is the **Bible basis** for each study. Whether it's just one verse or several chapters, the Bible basis reflects that the truths of Christian faith are contained in God's Word.

Each study brings the biblical point and the Bible basis to life with a **topic** relevant to young adults. People care about—and therefore like to talk and learn about—what's happening in their world at this moment. The topic brings their world, the Bible, and the point together to create a relevant, involving study of faith.

Background boxes throughout each study add insight to Scriptures, historical facts, or culture. **Leader tips** offer "coaching" suggestions on everything from altering activities for different-sized groups to alternative supplies. Plus, most studies include photocopiable **handouts** to use with your group.

How effective are the studies?

Young Adult Faith-Launchers uses active and interactive learning to vault students straight into the heart of the study. Most of us learn through experience. That's what active learning is all about. It gets everyone involved and lets people *do* what they're studying. They *feel* the effects of the principles—much like aircraft pilots *feel* the principles they're learning about velocity and angles when they use a flight simulator.

Interactive learning simply takes active learning a step further by having people teach each other what they've learned. It encourages people to work together, form relationships with others, and internalize and remember their discoveries.

Also, instead of using activity for activity's sake, *Young Adult Faith-Launchers* asks students tough questions to help them evaluate the active-learning experience. Small-group discussions help people interpret the experience, draw out its meaning, and relate the principles they learn to their lives.

Can students lead these studies?

Because the studies in *Young Adult Faith-Launchers* have all the information someone needs to present a compelling topic—including discussion questions, leader tips, and lists of supplies—the studies can be

Leader tip ▼

The studies generally run from forty-five to sixty-five minutes. At times, group discussions can take longer than you may have planned. If time's running short, simply choose and focus on the two or three questions from an activity you feel would best meet your group's needs. Also, when you ask groups to discuss a list of questions, write the list on newsprint and tape it to a wall so groups can discuss the questions at their own pace.

Leader tip ▾

Because these topics are so powerful and relevant to peoples' lives, your group members may be tempted to get caught up in issues and lose sight of the deeper principle found in the biblical point. Guide students to focus on the biblical investigation and to discuss how God's truth connects with reality in their lives.

peer-led. When people are given the responsibility to lead others, they take ownership of the class. Peer-led classes also encourage involvement because *everyone* becomes a leader and is encouraged to reach out to others.

How do I use *Young Adult Faith-Launchers*?

To begin, review the table of contents; there, you'll find the biblical point around which each study revolves. Or browse the topical or scriptural indexes to find a study about a topic or Scripture your group wants to deal with.

Once you've decided to do a study, read through it, study the Scriptures on which it's based, and read the background boxes and leader tips. Finally, gather the listed supplies. You're all set!

Looking Up

looking up

Absolute Truth

Discerning Right From Wrong

BIBLICAL POINT: God's holiness sets the standard for right and wrong.

BIBLE BASIS: Ephesians 4:17-24 and 1 Peter 1:13-21

TOPIC: Right and Wrong

introduction

Is truth dead? A researcher surveyed college men and found that one-third might rape a woman if they knew they wouldn't get caught.

Is truth dead? In the 1940s, less than a quarter of college students anonymously admitted to cheating in high school. Today three-quarters openly admit to cheating.

Is truth dead? When a Harvard student was asked to remove a Confederate flag that she had draped from her fourth-floor dormitory window, she refused, responding, "If they talk about diversity, they're gonna get it. If they talk about tolerance, they better be ready to have it."

Is truth dead? What would the people in your group say?

This study takes students on a journey into a world devoid of absolutes to help young adults discover the chaos that erupts when people deny the existence of absolute truth. Through this experience, students can learn that God's holiness sets the standard for right and wrong in all our lives.

Before the study, gather the following supplies:
- Bibles with concordances,
- newsprint,
- one "Absolute Truth" handout (p. 15) for every two people,
- tape,
- markers, and
- pencils.

■ Relational Taboo

(up to 5 minutes)

Supplies: Bibles, newsprint

After everyone has arrived, have students form pairs; then give each pair a two-by-two-foot sheet of newsprint to stand on. Once each pair is standing on its newsprint square, say: **Let's discover whether you and your partner see eye to eye on some important issues of right and wrong. I'm going to call out a series of statements. If *both* you and your partner**

absolute truth

● God's holiness sets the standard for right and wrong.

Leader tip ▼

If there's an uneven number of people in the group, you'll need to either find a partner and participate in this activity or have three people stand on a piece of newsprint together.

absolutely agree or absolutely disagree with the statement I call out, do nothing. But if *one* of you disagrees even a little with the statement, he or she must tear off half of the newsprint you're standing on together. Then you must try to stand together on the newsprint that remains.

Once everyone understands the instructions, read the statements below. After reading each statement, allow time for pairs to agree or disagree and to rip their newsprint squares if necessary. Call out the following statements one at a time:

● **Abortion is murder.**

● **It would be good to have a national death penalty for serious criminals.**

● **Sex before marriage is always wrong.**

● **A parent should be allowed to discipline a child by striking the child on the bottom.**

● **There is more than one path to eternal life.**

● **One person's idea of truth may not be the same as another person's.**

● **There is no such thing as absolute truth.**

After reading all the statements and allowing everyone to respond, have pairs discuss these questions:

● **Was this experience difficult? Why or why not?**

● **How was standing together on the newsprint similar to sharing common beliefs about right and wrong?**

● **What happened as the newsprint got smaller?**

● **How would you compare that experience to losing "common ground" when your beliefs about right and wrong change?**

● **Do you think there is an absolute right or wrong for any of the issues we mentioned? Why or why not?**

● **Can we be sure that any action or attitude is always right or always wrong? Why or why not?**

● **Does anyone have the authority to decide what's right or wrong for everyone? Why or why not?**

Ask for a couple of volunteers to read aloud Ephesians 4:17-24 and 1 Peter 1:13-21. Then have pairs discuss the following questions:

● **What do these Scriptures say about God?**

● **What do these Scriptures say about how we should act? why we should act that way?**

● **Why do you think this was an important message for the early church?**

● **Do you think this is an important message for each of us today? Why or why not?**

Say: **Many people today believe that deciding right from wrong is a personal issue. And to a degree, that's a healthy perspective. After all, it's not up to me to tell you whether you should wear purple pants or change your name to Englebert Jones. But there are some actions and attitudes in life that are always wrong. How do I know?**

Helping Students Understand Right From Wrong

Many young adults live in a world without moral absolutes. So how can you impact those students with absolute truth? Try these suggestions:

1. Examine moral relativism with students. You can begin by leading this study. But be warned! Even when you point out that believing in moral relativism means that no one can ever be wrong, your students may argue that society at large can determine what's right and wrong for the people within it. Your students might say, "Murder is wrong in this country because most people in our society believe it's wrong. And, in the same way, abortion is legal because the majority of people think it's OK."

If students raise this argument, ask them about Nazism, Hitler, and the Holocaust. Hitler's Germany believed it was "right" to extinguish the Jews from the face of the earth. In a relativistic world, the Nazis wouldn't be condemned for this belief, and yet they were. Why? Was their society "wrong"? And if a society can be wrong, how can I trust that my society is right when it says abortion is OK?

2. Focus people on the need for trust in relationships. In a world without absolutes, nothing and no one can be trusted absolutely. Betrayal—not commitment—is the norm for relationships. For example, the research of Christian pollster George Barna showed that four out of five teenagers rank "having one marriage partner for life" as "very desirable." But in a world without moral absolutes, what happens if the marriage is no longer "right for me"? In that case, staying in the marriage would become the "wrong" thing to do, regardless of my partner's desires.

3. Encourage students toward a closer personal relationship with Jesus. Because Jesus *is* the Truth, encourage your students to get to know him better. The more time they spend with him and in his Word, the more willing they'll become to accept Christ's holiness as the standard for right and wrong.

4. Point students to God's "bottom line." Today's young adults have been called the Bottom-Line Generation, and for good reason. They know they'll have to sacrifice a great deal to fix the problems they've inherited from their elders: drugs, war, poverty, the national debt, Social Security shortfall, welfare fraud, educational failures, pollution—the list goes on. When confronted with these issues, they'll typically respond with gritty realism. "Just tell us how much it's going to cost," they say. And then they're willing to pay it.

That mind-set can also help them understand the unchangeable nature of moral absolutes. God is God, and he has set up certain moral absolutes that cannot be circumvented or ignored—any more than gravity can be suspended. God's moral absolutes are a reality of life on earth, and we have to learn to honor them on a daily basis. Your students should understand language like that. So don't be skittish about telling them God's bottom line. It's the language of the real world.

Because God's holiness sets the standard for right and wrong. By examining what God says is holy or profane, I can tell whether something is right or wrong for me—and for everyone else.

■ Absolute Confusion

(35 to 40 minutes)
Supplies: Newsprint, markers, tape

Say: **We all believe in absolute truth whether we admit it or not. How do I know? Because without absolute truth, life would be nothing but chaos. Let's do a fun experiment to demonstrate that we all believe in absolute truth.**

Have people form teams of four to six. Then set out chairs, newsprint, markers, and tape. Say: **In a moment, teams are going to take turns building altars to God. When it's your team's turn, the rest of the group will tell your team members how they are related to each other and where the altar construction will take place. For instance, the group might say, "You're all sailors on a life raft in the Pacific Ocean." Then your team must construct an altar as if you're sailors stuck on a life raft.**

But that's not all. As each team takes its turn, I'll change the "laws of reality" by calling out new right-and-wrong beliefs that teams also must act out. For example, if I say, "Cheating is good," then all the team members must try to cheat each other as they work on building their altar.

Once teams understand the instructions, choose a team to go first. Have the rest of the group decide how the team members should be related and where the action should take place. For example, team members could be members of the Mafia on a drug plane, or they could be family members who work together as trapeze artists in a circus. Allow the team to work for three minutes, using the supplies you set out to create an altar. When time is up, stop the action and allow another team to construct an altar. Once again, have the group decide on a location and on how all the team members are related. Continue until all the teams have had a chance to work.

As each team works on its altar, change the "laws of reality" by calling out one of the statements below. Call out a new statement every thirty seconds or so. It's OK to repeat some laws more than once. Here are the laws:

- **No one else matters except you.**
- **Destroying trees or wildlife is a sin worthy of death.**
- **Hate makes you powerful.**
- **You are all gods.**
- **The person who's wearing the most red is a god.**
- **Cheating is good.**
- **You can never tell another person what to do.**

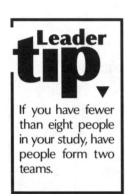

Leader tip

If you have fewer than eight people in your study, have people form two teams.

■ Debriefing

(5 to 10 minutes)

Supplies: Bibles with concordances, pencils, "Absolute Truth" handouts (p. 15), tape, newsprint, markers

(p. 15)

After all the teams have had a chance to build their altars, have students form pairs. Give each pair a pencil and an "Absolute Truth" handout. Make sure each pair has access to a Bible with a good concordance. Say: **Go through the handout with your partner. Use a Bible and a concordance to help you discover at least five absolute truths that counter many of the false beliefs we heard in the last activity.**

As pairs work, tape a sheet of newsprint to a wall, and set out several markers. As pairs finish, have them write on the newsprint each of the truths they discovered, along with the Bible passages they used to validate each truth.

Say: **Who would've thought there were so many absolute truths in life? If we listen to many of the voices in the world, we may start to believe that there is no such thing as absolute truth. But because we know God, we know better. God's holiness sets the standard for right and wrong. God defines absolute truth and shows us how to live as we should.**

You may want to write on newsprint the false beliefs you called out in the previous activity. Hang up the newsprint, and have pairs write their biblically based absolute truths next to the false beliefs.

■ Prayer Experience

(5 to 10 minutes)

Supplies: None needed

Say: **Absolute truth can be hard to swallow because sometimes we all want to do our own thing in our own way. But absolute truth is kind of like God's "bottom line." There's no way around it. We have to humble ourselves and recognize that in many situations, we don't define what's right and wrong. God's holiness sets that standard for us.**

Have each student find a new partner to discuss these questions:

● **Are you willing to submit to God's absolute truth as it's explained in Scripture? Why or why not?**

● **What's one absolute truth that your partner demonstrates well?**

● **What's one truth you want to learn to submit to better in your own life?**

Have partners pray for each other, asking for God to grant them the humility to submit to his truth and to let his truth guide their choices in daily life.

Understanding Relativism

The popular belief that you can build your own reality—and therefore, define your own truth—has created for young adults an entire culture of relativism. Relativism says, in essence, "If it works for you, it must be good. I have no right to judge your choices. I can only make choices for myself." Nobody has to believe the same things, do the same things, or think the same way. Each person can be the master of his or her own fate because no one can know what's right (or wrong) for anyone better than himself or herself.

This may all sound reasonable and even respectful on the surface, but such a relativistic belief has one fatal flaw: Without an external, self-existent standard of absolute truth, no one's actions can ever be truly deemed "wrong" or even "inappropriate." If I feel like loving you today, that's OK. But if I get up tomorrow and decide to kill you, that's got to be OK, too. After all, with no absolute standard of right and wrong, who can judge me?

That fatal flaw in relativistic thought offers the strongest argument for God's holy standard of absolute truth. Young adults want beliefs that'll work for them in the real world every day. Ultimately, relativism *doesn't* work. It's neither practical nor true. When your students see that, it won't be long before they abandon their relativistic beliefs for something better—God's absolute truth.

(Portions of this study are adapted from "Teaching Black-and-White Truths to Gray-Minded Kids," Michael Warden, GROUP Magazine, September/October 1995.)

"You were taught, with regard to your former way of life, to put off your old self, which is being corrupted by its deceitful desires; to be made new in the attitude of your minds; and to put on the new self, created to be like God in true righteousness and holiness."

– Ephesians 4:22-24

Absolute Truth

h a n d o u t

Discuss These Questions:

- What's your reaction to the altar-building activity?

- Was it difficult trying to build an altar while the "laws of reality" kept changing? Why or why not?

- How is that experience similar to what it would be like to follow God in a world with no absolutes?

- What would the world be like if there really were no such thing as absolute truth?

- What's one absolute truth that you believe and try to live out in your life?

- How do you know your belief really is an absolute truth and not just your own opinion?

We all have opinions, but we can tell whether an opinion is absolute truth by looking in the Bible. God's Word describes for us God's holy character. And God's holiness sets the standard for right and wrong in our lives.

Examine the list of false beliefs you encountered in the altar-building activity. Then use a Bible and a concordance to find one or more absolute truths in Scripture that nullify each false belief.

Here are the false beliefs you heard in the altar-building activity:

- No one else matters except you.

- Destroying trees or wildlife is a sin worthy of death.

- Hate makes you powerful.

- You are all gods.

- The person who's wearing the most red is a god.

- Cheating is good.

- You can never tell another person what to do.

In this space, write the Scripture passages and absolute truths you discover:

Cult Repellent

Recognizing the Lure of Cults

BIBLICAL POINT: Faith in Jesus is the only way to eternal life.

BIBLE BASIS: Matthew 7:15-23; John 3:16-18; 14:6-7; and 1 Timothy 2:5-6

TOPIC: Cults

Young adults today lost their naiveté at a young age. For years they've been taught through school, the media, and their own experiences about gangs, drugs, abuse, sexually transmitted diseases, and a thousand other threats to safety and happiness.

However, for all their street smarts, many young adults are oblivious to one threat that's just as dangerous as a gun to the head or a needle in the arm: cults.

These days most cult members don't shave their heads, wear strange robes, or stand on street corners chanting mantras. In most cases, today's cult member looks, thinks, and acts just like you.

And your group members.

This study unmasks cults and cult leaders so young adults can recognize counterfeit beliefs about salvation and the church, and recognize cult leaders as the false prophets Jesus warned about. Through this study, students will discover the truth that faith in Jesus is the only way to eternal life.

Before the study, gather various articles of clothing or materials such as towels or bedsheets that groups can use to create costumes.
You'll also need

● Bibles,
● a "Cult Clues" handout (p. 23) for each person,
● paper,
● pencils,
● index cards,
● masking tape,
● markers, and
● newsprint.

cult repellent
● Faith in Jesus is the only way to eternal life.

■ Group Transformation

(10 to 15 minutes)

Supplies: A Bible, paper, pencils, various clothing items

Have people form three groups, and have each group select a "recorder." Give each recorder a sheet of paper and a pencil. Instruct group members to brainstorm about words and phrases that define what a cult is or describe what a cult does. Tell recorders to write down everyone's ideas.

After a few minutes, set out the various articles of clothing you collected before the session. Then say: **Based on the information you've come up with, I want you to transform your entire group into a cult. Choose a "cult leader" from among your group members, and decide what characteristics or practices will make your group an official cult. You can use any of the supplies I've provided or anything else in the room to help you transform yourselves.**

Give groups several minutes to transform; then have groups take turns presenting themselves to the rest of the students. Have students guess what makes each group a "true cult."

After groups present their transformations, have students form trios that include one person from each group. Have trios discuss the following questions:

● **How were our presentations of cults similar? different?**

● **How hard is it to recognize a cult when you encounter one?**

● **How would you respond if you were asked to join a cult? Why?**

● **Why do you think people join cults?**

Say: **As you discussed, people join cults for many reasons. Some people think they'll find friends or a new, improved family. Some people are searching for meaning in life. Some people think they'll find power or eternal benefits.**

Ask a volunteer to read aloud John 3:16-18. Then say: **Since faith in Jesus is the *only* way to eternal life, we should avoid organizations that claim there are other ways to know God. However, that's not always as easy as it sounds. Jesus taught that some cults and cult leaders are much harder to spot than the ones you've just portrayed. So today we're going to learn how to recognize a cult when we see one.**

Leader tip

If you have fewer than ten students, you may want to have students form two groups for this activity rather than three. If you have more than thirty students, you might consider forming six groups instead of three.

Adjusting the size of the groups will allow students to participate more fully in the discussions and activities. However, if you choose to adjust the size of the groups, be sure to adjust the activities throughout the study accordingly.

What Makes a Cult?

Christians often identify cults on the basis of their deviation from the theological truths taught in the Bible. Unfortunately, this approach to cult identification fails as often as it succeeds. Many cults claim to have the correct interpretation of the Bible, so the battle for truth is reduced to endless bickering over interpretations. Also, most "theological" definitions of "cult" neglect the fact that cults often inflict significant psychological and social damage on their members. Therefore, instead of focusing on a theological definition, this study examines typical cult behavior. This approach teaches kids to identify cults by their actions as well as by their beliefs.

In terms of theology, many cults appear to be genuinely Christian. However, cults inevitably distort, deny, or add to some part of Christian truth. Also, cults often employ various methods of manipulation to destroy members' self-identity and to control thoughts and actions. Even as cults promise to meet members' social needs through nurturing relationships and a caring environment, they also pressure members to isolate themselves from family members, friends, and society.

Describing cults in these terms can help young adults recognize the different ways any group can be cultic. Some groups may be socially nurturing but theologically incorrect; others may be theologically sound but psychologically damaging. In either case, young adults need to beware of the cultic tendencies of all the groups they encounter.

■ You Can't Trust Everyone

(10 to 15 minutes)

Supplies: Bibles, index cards, pencils

Have people re-form their three original groups. Give everyone an index card and a pencil. Assign one of the following questions to each group:

● **How are false prophets like true prophets? different from true prophets?**

● **What kinds of bad "fruit" will we see in false prophets?**

● **What may be the consequences of trusting a false prophet?**

Instruct the groups to read Matthew 7:15-23 and discuss how the biblical passage answers their assigned questions. Have everyone jot down ideas from the discussions so they can report what they learn to members of other groups.

After two minutes, have students re-form the trios from the "Group Transformation" discussion. Tell each person to take thirty seconds to explain how the biblical passage answers his or her assigned question. After everyone has reported, have trios discuss the following questions:

● **How are cult leaders like false prophets? different?**

● **How might cult leaders seem similar to true Christian leaders? different from true Christian leaders?**

● **How can we recognize a cult leader when we see one?**

● **What might be the consequences of following a cult leader?**

Say: **The cult leaders of today, like the false prophets of Jesus' day, are sometimes difficult to spot. Cult leaders often look and act like Christians, but they secretly distort the foundational Christian belief that faith in Jesus is the only way to eternal life. That's why we need to know how to see through a cult leader's positive image to the negative reality that lurks under the surface.**

Biblical Background

n Matthew 7:15-23, Jesus uses two metaphors to teach his listeners how to recognize false prophets.

First, false prophets are like ferocious wolves dressed in sheep's clothing. They may look like one of the flock from a distance, but closer scrutiny and time always reveal the wolves' true identities. It's their nature to act like wolves, and eventually they'll try to consume the sheep.

Second, false prophets are like thornbushes and thistles that can't produce edible fruit. Although the berries on the buckthorn may resemble grapes and the flowers on certain thistles may look like blooming figs, closer inspection reveals that these plants bear only "bad fruit."

Jesus' point is that we must carefully and patiently examine leaders to discern their true nature and the "fruit" that their nature produces.

■ Looks May Be Deceiving

(15 to 20 minutes)

Supplies: "Cult Clues" handouts (p. 23)

Have students return to their three original groups. Give each person a photocopy of the "Cult Clues" handout. Read aloud the summary at the top of the handout, and then assign each group one section of the handout. Say: **Your first cult transformation was based on your own impressions of what cults are like. Now I want you to transform your group into a new cult. This time, base your group's transformation on the information provided in your assigned section of the handout.**

Give groups several minutes to prepare, and then have groups take turns presenting themselves to the rest of the students. As groups make their presentations, ask them to explain how their cult reflects the information in the handout.

Once the presentations are finished, have everyone return to the trios to discuss these questions:

● How were these transformations like the earlier ones? different from the earlier ones?

● Based on what you've learned, how would you define "cult"?

● How do cults appear to be Christian?

● How are cults different from true Christianity?

● Which cult characteristics would be attractive to your friends?

● What bad "fruit" can you look for in organizations to learn whether they might be cultic?

Say: **Cult leaders often set themselves up as equal—or even superior—to Jesus. But cult leaders are never able to offer us true salvation. Ultimately, they always fail to deliver what they promise. That's because faith in Jesus is the only way to eternal life.**

■ Creative Comparison

(5 to 10 minutes)

Supplies: Bibles, index cards, pencil, masking tape, marker

Ask for a volunteer "cult leader" to stand where everyone can see him or her. Have people call out any negative characteristics of cult leaders they've discovered during the study. For example, someone might say, "Cult leaders tell lies" or "Cult leaders take advantage of people." Write each characteristic on an index card, and tape it to the cult leader. After people call out five or six characteristics, instruct half the study group to read John 14:6-7 and the other half to read 1 Timothy 2:5-6.

After students read their passages, ask for a volunteer "Jesus" to stand beside the cult leader. Have people call out positive qualities of Jesus—based on the Scripture passages—that cancel out the cult leader's negative characteristics. For example, someone might say, "Jesus is the truth" or "Jesus works for our benefit." Each time someone calls out a positive quality, remove the index card with the corresponding negative characteristic from the cult leader, cross out the negative characteristic with a marker, write the positive quality on an index card, and tape it to "Jesus." Have people call out positive qualities of Jesus until every negative characteristic of the cult leader has been canceled out.

Say: **Cults and cult leaders often claim that they hold the key to a deeper relationship with God. But once you compare cult leaders with Jesus, the truth becomes clear: Faith in Jesus is the only way to eternal life.**

Thank the volunteers, and have "Jesus" remove the index cards from his or her clothing.

Groups will probably act out the second transformation in their normal clothes. However, if one or more of the groups creates costumes for the second transformation, have each of the three groups discuss whether they'll really be able to recognize cult members by the way they dress or behave in public.

If someone identifies a positive quality of Jesus that doesn't correspond to any of the negative characteristics, simply write the quality on an index card, and tape it to "Jesus."

■ Helping a Friend

(up to 5 minutes)

Supplies: newsprint, tape, markers

Ask the entire group to brainstorm about ways people might help a friend who's been lured into a cult. Tape up a sheet of newsprint, and record everyone's ideas on it.

Then distribute markers, and have each person write a short prayer on the newsprint for their specific needs. For example, some students might want God to show them how to help their friends, while others might want God to help them recognize and resist the lure of cults.

After everyone is finished writing a prayer, close the meeting with a spoken prayer, asking God to protect people from the deception of cults and thanking him for sending Jesus, the only true source of eternal life.

How to Help Someone Who's in a Cult

Getting someone out of a cult can be a long, difficult process that requires great patience and love. Strategies for "intervention" abound, but the most effective approaches always include these ground rules:

- Don't panic or become angry at the person you're trying to help.
- Educate yourself about the specific beliefs and practices of the cult.
- Enlist the aid of former members of the cult, church leaders, and counselors with experience in cult intervention.
- Offer unconditional love and acceptance to the person you're trying to win back.
- Rely upon God for strength, guidance, and the success of your spiritual battle.

For additional information on cults or helping someone who's in a cult, see *The Lure of the Cults and New Religions* by Ronald M. Enroth and *Combatting Cult Mind Control* by Steve Hassan.

"Jesus answered, 'I am the way and the truth and the life. No one comes to the Father except through me.'"

—John 14:6

Cult Clues

handout

Cult members don't always wear strange outfits, distribute literature in airports, or stand on street corners and chant. In fact, most cults are a confused and confusing mix of truth and error, good and bad. Cults are often appealing precisely because they appear to be genuine expressions of true Christianity, but they're ultimately based on damaging lies. The following clues will help you recognize a cult when you see one.

Social Traits
Cults...

• pressure members to break ties with friends and family;

• offer love, support, and friendship to people in crises;

• enforce strict rules about eating, sleeping, and free time;

• may organize into a church or "Christian" ministry;

• require members to support and obey a spiritual leader; and

• threaten to expel members who don't follow cult standards.

Theological Traits
Cults...

• may accept, teach, and promote some Christian beliefs;

• often distort or deny Christian beliefs about Christ;

• emphasize spiritual commitment and service;

• substitute study of cult literature for Bible study;

• appeal to people seeking a deeper relationship with God; and

• claim to be the only ones who understand the truth.

Psychological Traits
Cults...

• manipulate people through guilt and fear of judgment;

• provide simple answers to life's complex questions;

• control every area of members' thoughts and lives;

• don't allow members to question the leader's authority;

• offer structure, stability, and security to members; and

• discourage individual freedom and self-expression.

Jesus Christ: Myth vs. Reality

BIBLICAL POINT: The Bible can show you the real Jesus.

BIBLE BASIS: Matthew 8:23-32; 9:35-36; 28:1-10; Luke 1:26-38; 2:1-20; John 1:1-14; 14:6-9

TOPIC: Jesus Christ

introduction

Who *is* Jesus, anyway? Even people who've been attending church their whole lives ponder this question. They can find many answers, too, and from great minds all over the world: "Jesus was a good man" "...a great teacher" "...an advanced soul" "...a prophet" "...a feminist" "...a fictional character" "...a political revolutionary" "...a failure."

Everyone seems ready to spout opinions, but the truth about Christ's personality and purpose still remains a mystery to most of the world.

And, possibly, to your students.

In this study, people will create their own representations of Jesus and examine portrayals of Jesus from magazines, from scholarly circles, and from the Bible. Through this examination, they'll discover that, despite the myriad of public opinions, there's one reliable place they can go to discover the real Jesus—the Bible.

 Before the study, write these questions on newsprint, and tape the newsprint to a wall:

- How can someone really get to know you?
- Who really knows you well?
- Do you believe that Jesus really knows you? Why or why not?
- How well do you know Jesus? Explain.

You'll also need

- Bibles;
- newsprint;
- markers;
- tape;
- copies of Newsweek, People, and Rolling Stone magazines;
- one photocopy each of the "Real Jesus" and the "Scholars Say..." handouts (pp. 30-31).

Jesus Christ: myth vs. reality

● The Bible can show you the real Jesus.

■ Getting to Know You

(up to 5 minutes)

Supplies: Newsprint, tape, a marker

As people arrive, have them form pairs to discuss the first question on the sheet of newsprint you taped to the wall before the study. After one minute, have people find new partners to discuss the second question. Continue until everyone has discussed all the questions.

Young Adults' Perspective

When it comes to God, Jesus, and Christianity, just what does the majority of young adults believe to be the truth? In his research-based book *Baby Busters: Disillusioned Generation*, George Barna lists some of the firmly held religious beliefs of today's young adults. Here's a sampling:

Belief Statement	Percentage of People Who Strongly Agree
There is only one God; he created the universe and rules it today.	66%
Jesus Christ, who is God's Son, rose from the dead and is alive today.	50%
The Bible is the Word of God and is totally accurate in all that it teaches.	44%
Christians, Jews, Buddhists, Muslims, and all others pray to the same god, even though they use different names for that god.	33%
All good people will go to heaven when they die.	27%
The Christian faith has all the answers to leading a successful life.	23%

■ Create Your Own Jesus

(15 to 20 minutes)

Supplies: Newsprint, markers, tape

Have the students form three groups, and give each group a set of colored markers and a "supersize" sheet of newsprint. Have each group trace the outline of one group member onto the newsprint. Say: **Now we're going to do a little creating. Think about this question:**

● **If you could create your own "custom" Jesus who would be with you throughout your life, what would he be like?**

In your group, work together to create a portrait of your custom Jesus. Draw features on the body, write character traits inside the outline, or draw symbols or pictures of how this Jesus would act. Limit yourselves to seven or fewer ideas. When all the drawings are ready, we'll tape them to a wall and create a "Jesus Portrait Gallery."

When groups have finished, have them tape their portraits of Jesus to a wall and explain their portraits to everyone. Remind groups not to criticize each other's presentations or artwork. Then ask:

● **How did you feel working with your group to create your own custom Jesus?**

● **Did you agree with all of your group members' suggestions for what Jesus should be like? Why or why not?**

● **How are our perceptions of Jesus alike? different?**

● **How was this activity similar to how people react to the true Jesus?**

Say: **Today we're going to take a close look at different people's opinions of who Jesus is. Through our investigation, we'll try to discover how we can know the real Jesus. Right now, find a partner and pray together, asking God to guide our group as we examine what different people say about Jesus.**

■ Who Do They Say He Is?

(25 to 30 minutes)

Supplies: Bibles; newsprint; tape; markers; copies of Newsweek, People, and Rolling Stone magazines; "The Real Jesus" and "The Scholars Say..." handouts (pp. 30-31)

Have people re-form the three groups from the previous activity. Give each group another supersize sheet of newsprint, and have each group trace a different group member's outline on the paper. Then give each group one of the following sets of materials:

    Set 1: One copy each of Newsweek, Rolling Stone, and People magazines

    Set 2: A photocopy of the "Scholars Say..." handout

    Set 3: A photocopy of the "Real Jesus" handout

Leader tip ▼

If you have more than thirty students, have them form six groups instead of three. This will make the study flow more smoothly when these same groups work together during the "Who Do They Say He Is?" activity.

Leader tip ▼

Some of the students in your study may not know Jesus at all, and their portrayals of Jesus and their answers to questions may indicate that. Be sure not to criticize these students' answers; instead, ask follow-up questions and guide them through the study, encouraging them to discover the truth about who Jesus really is. Then, at the end of the study, let everyone know that you'd be happy to discuss (now or later) questions people have about Jesus.

Say: **Using only the information I've given you, create a new picture of Jesus that illustrates what your information teaches. For example, if your information describes Jesus as a radical feminist, you could draw him with a women's-rights picket sign in his hand. Give your Jesus portrait a title based on the source of your information. When you're finished, we'll add your new Jesus to our Jesus Portrait Gallery.**

While groups are working, copy the biblical passages from the "Real Jesus" handout onto newsprint so everyone can see them. The whole group will use them later in the study.

After fifteen to twenty minutes, have groups tape their new portraits to the "gallery" wall. Say: **There are a lot of different images of Jesus portrayed in our world. But let's see how we can figure out who the real Jesus is.**

■ Art Critiques

(5 to 10 minutes)
Supplies: Bibles, newsprint

Have students form trios consisting of one person from each of the previous study groups. Have each group choose an "asker" to keep everyone focused on the questions, a "recorder" to keep track of the discussion, and a "reporter" to share the group's conclusions with the rest of the study. Say: **Now you're going to be art critics. In your trios, discuss what's real and what's illusory about each of these portrayals of Jesus. Look at the passages of Scripture I've written on this piece of newsprint** (point to the newsprint you taped to a wall during the previous activity) **to help you. Also, use these questions to guide your discussion as you look at each drawing:**

● **How is the depiction like or unlike the real Jesus?**

● **How is the depiction like an advertisement—an illusion someone is trying to sell to our society?**

● **How could the Bible help someone decide whether this depiction represents the real Jesus?**

Allow trios a few minutes to critique each newsprint portrait. After all trios have finished examining the portraits, have the reporters share what they discussed with the rest of the study.

Then ask:

● **From these portraits, how do you think people can find an accurate depiction of who Jesus really is? Explain.**

Say: **Many people portray Jesus with images and opinions that seem contrary to one another. Fortunately, God has provided a true picture of who Jesus really is through the Bible.** Ask:

● **Has your picture of Jesus changed since the beginning of the study? Why or why not?**

● **How has the opinion of other people or our culture affected the way you see Jesus? Explain.**

- How can you "test" whether or not those opinions are accurate?
- How can you ensure that you will be able to spot false portrayals of Jesus and counter them in your life or your friends' lives?
- Why is the Bible such an important part of helping you understand the real Jesus?

Have people find partners to discuss these final questions:

- How would understanding and believing in the real Jesus change the way you live?
- What's one thing you'll do this week to understand the real Jesus better?

Have pairs close by praying together, asking God to help them grow in their understanding and commitment to the real Jesus.

Cultural Portraits

One form of media that has affected young adults more than any previous generation is television. And television often doesn't present a positive or accurate image of Jesus. In a study titled *Watching America,* Professor Stanley Rothman showed that instead of reflecting a realistic picture of American beliefs, television typically reflects the biases and views of those who create the programming.

For example, 93 percent of television's creative leaders say they never or seldom attend religious services. More than 50 percent of that same group claim that God plays no role in society today. In fact, many television industry leaders say that the influence of religion and God on society has been "detrimental."

Has that message gotten through to your students?

"In the beginning was the Word, and the Word was with God, and the Word was God. He was with God in the beginning. Through him all things were made; without him nothing was made that has been made. In him was life, and that life was the light of men. The light shines in the darkness, but the darkness has not understood it."

—John 1:1–5

The Real Jesus

handout

Let these passages help you gain a clearer picture of the real Jesus according to the Bible:

Matthew 8:23-32—Jesus demonstrated power over both the natural world and the spiritual world by calming the storm and driving out demons. It's interesting to note that Jesus' disciples wondered who he really was, but the demons recognized him immediately as the Son of God.

Matthew 9:35-36—Jesus wasn't just bent on demonstrating his mighty power; he was a man of compassion. Though his teachings were important, he always had enough time—and love—to take care of hurting people.

Matthew 28:1-10—Jesus' death on the cross wasn't an unexpected tragedy but part of a glorious plan to defeat death. Notice that the first to hear of Jesus' resurrection and to see him were women—second-class citizens in the culture of that day.

Luke 1:26-38; 2:1-20—Jesus' birth was announced to Mary through an angel who made it clear that Jesus would be supernaturally conceived—without doubt the Son of God. And when Jesus was born, God sent angels to deliver the birth announcement to earth. Shepherds—considered some of the lowliest people on earth—were the first to hear that the Savior had been born.

John 1:1-14—Jesus has existed forever. He was with God and was active in creation. The term "Word," referring to Jesus, carries a much deeper meaning than the "Word of God" as we think of it. In the original Greek, the word means unique thoughts that powerfully convey the mind of the author. Thus, in Jesus, God has shown us himself.

John 14:6-9—Jesus made it clear that he is the only way through which we can have a relationship with the Father. In fact, he claims divinity, insisting that the Father is in him and that he is in the Father.

The Scholars Say...

h a n d o u t

"There was no such person in the history of the world as Jesus Christ. There was no historical, living, breathing, sentient human being by that name. Ever. [The Bible] is a fictional, non-historical narrative. The myth is good for business."

—Jon Murray, President of American Atheists

"Muslims see him as the greatest prophet before the prophet of Islam. He is the prophet of inward spiritual life.

"Islam does not accept that he was crucified, died, then was resurrected. Islam believes he was taken to heaven without dying, without suffering the pain of death."

—Seyyed Hossein Nasr, Professor of Islamic studies at George Washington University

"Greek Orthodox theologians say the main purpose of Jesus was to bring God and man closer, but not necessarily to die in that atoning way we've developed in the West. Their favorite image of Jesus is not the crucified figure but the transfigured, when the divinity shines through him, rather like the image of Buddha sitting under the bo tree—the example of a deified humanity, which we shall all be like one day."

—Karen Armstrong, Professor of Religion at Leo Baeck College, author of *A History of God*

"Jesus, to succeed, had to choose martyrdom. He had been a failure in all sorts of human enterprises. One was to convert everybody to love, to turning the other cheek. He was an abysmal failure at that. He was also a failure in his more militant role—scourging the moneylenders, and so forth. He changed nothing. So, basically, the only power he had at the end was the power of abdication."

—Peter A. Bien, professor of English at Dartmouth College, translator of *The Last Temptation of Christ*

"He was a feminist. He cured ill women, allowed them to become people who related his truths, forgave a repentant prostitute, allowed her to touch him. Women gave their money to support him. Mary Magdalen was the first witness to the Resurrection—what's more important than that, in Christianity? She was apostle to the apostles, told by Christ to go tell them he had risen."

—Susan Haskins, author of *Mary Magdalen: Myth and Metaphor*

The above quotations are excerpted from Life magazine, December 1994.

"I Just Can't Wait!"

Understanding the Need for Patience

BIBLICAL POINT: The Holy Spirit helps us wait for what's best.

BIBLE BASIS: Genesis 15:1-6; 16:1-12; 21:1-21; and Acts 16:6-40

TOPIC: Instant Gratification

introduction

"**B**ut, Daddy, I want a golden goose, and I want it *now!*"

Most of us can relate to Veruca Salt's plea in the movie *Willie Wonka and the Chocolate Factory*. Not only do we know what we want, we want it immediately.

Of course, our society caters to this desire. Remote controls, microwaves, drive-through windows, e-mail, and real-time computer chats with people around the world have conditioned us to get what we want when we want it. Think about it: When's the last time you impatiently tapped your toe because your computer printer didn't spit out a document within ten seconds?

This is the context young adults have experienced as they've grown up. They're used to instant breakfasts, instant coffees, instant cures. Many haven't learned the discipline of delaying gratification, of waiting for what's best.

This study will invite students to develop that discipline—to rely on the Holy Spirit for patience in all areas of their lives.

Before the study, make a copy of the "Quiet Zone!" handout (p. 39), and tape the handout to a wall of your meeting room. You'll also need

- Bibles,
- one "How Long..." handout (p. 40) for every three students,
- one "Abram's Wait" handout (p. 41) for each person,
- pencils,
- masking tape, and
- paper.

"i just can't wait!"
● The Holy Spirit helps us wait for what's best.

■ Wait Station

(5 to 10 minutes)

Supplies: "Quiet Zone!" handout (p. 39), tape

As students arrive, silently direct them toward the "Quiet Zone!" handout on the wall. Allow the silence to continue until you're five minutes into your meeting time. Then have students form trios to discuss these questions:

● **What's your reaction to starting our meeting with silent time?**

● **What were you thinking and feeling as you waited for our meeting to start?**

● **What do you usually do when you're waiting for something or someone?**

● **What's the longest time you've ever spent waiting for something? How did you react to waiting in that situation?**

● **Do you think anything good can come from waiting for something? Why or why not?**

● **What is our culture's view of waiting? Why do you think our culture is that way?**

Say: **Today we're going to talk about instant gratification and how seeking it can cause us to miss out on some great stuff in life. The Holy Spirit helps us wait for what's best, and we're going to learn a bit about patience as this study goes on.**

■ Test of Patience

(15 to 20 minutes)

Supplies: Bibles, "How Long..." handouts (p. 40), pencils, "Abram's Wait" handouts (p. 41)

Have people remain in their trios. Hand each trio a "How Long…" handout and a pencil. Say: **To begin our discussion on waiting, let's take a quick quiz about how long some things have taken. In your trios, go through the handout, and as a team take your best guesses for each item on the quiz. You have five minutes.**

After five minutes or when all the groups have finished the quiz, read aloud the information in the "Answers" box on page 35, and have trios tally their correct answers. If you wish, find out which trio had the most correct answers. Then ask:

● **Did the length of any of the events on the quiz surprise you? If so, which ones and why?**

● **How would you respond if you had to wait as long as some of these people (and animals) to achieve what you set out to do? Explain.**

Answers

1. c

2. d

3. d

4. d

5. b (Andreas Mihavecz of Austria was put in a holding cell in a local government building and then forgotten by police for eighteen days.)

6. d (Iris Haughie Johns and Aro Haughie Campbell were reunited after seventy-five years by the New Zealand TV show *Missing.*)

7. d (Second Steward Poon Lim's ship was torpedoed, and after 133 days he was picked up by a fishing boat off the coast of Brazil.)

8. a

9. c

10. d

11. Answers will vary.

Say: **As we can see from this quiz and as we know from our own lives, we have to wait patiently for many things. But waiting can be really difficult. When we really want something, we want it instantaneously.**

Abram, a man who lived in Old Testament times, also struggled with patience. Let's explore his story.

Hand each student a photocopy of the "Abram's Wait" handout. Have trios go through the handout together.

When trios have finished their discussions, invite them to share their answers to some of the questions on the handout. Then say: **While Abram (later Abraham) showed some haste in his actions, things didn't turn out all bad. He gained two sons. But life became much more difficult than it would have if he had waited, knowing that God would fulfill his promise. The Holy Spirit helps us wait for what's best.**

Leader tip

If you have six or fewer students, still create a masking tape box and have people stand in it. But also tape three or four lines within the box to serve as permanent "walls" that people cannot go through to reach the end. Have one person run through the maze at a time. If possible give each person a chance to run through it. For added incentive, time the participants to see who can get through the maze the fastest.

▪ Changing Circumstances

(20 to 25 minutes)

Supplies: Bibles, masking tape, paper, pencils

Say: **Sometimes the Holy Spirit makes us wait for what's best because he's creating the best situation for us, one that wouldn't happen if we rushed straight into what we want. Let's play a game to explore this.**

Recruit two volunteers, then have the rest of the students form at least four even lines. Have them extend their arms to their sides, making sure they have an arm's length between them and the people around them (everyone's hands should reach the shoulders of the people all around them). Then have the two volunteers help you quickly create a masking tape rectangle on the floor around the lines of people. Make sure the lines are an arm's length from the people on the edges. Then have one volunteer stand at one corner and the other stand at any other corner.

Say: **The object of this game is for our volunteers to get to the corner opposite from them diagonally. But to do that, they must go through the rest of you. They cannot step out of the masking tape lines. They must go through the paths you make with your bodies as you stand there with your arms stretched out to the sides. However, you'll change the configuration of the pathways. Whenever I say "change," turn your body to face another line. It can be the line to your left, right, or even to your back. Keep your arms extended! We'll do this until our volunteers reach their destinations.**

Begin the game with students facing any line they wish to face and having their arms outstretched. Allow the volunteers to begin their run. About every ten seconds, yell "change." Continue to do this until both volunteers reach their destinations. Play the game as many rounds as your time allows.

After the game, ask:

● **What's your reaction to this game?**

● **How is this game like waiting for something you want in life? How is it different?**

● **What is something you've waited for recently that you've had to wade through obstacles to get? In that situation, did the waiting have a good or a bad consequence? Explain.**

Have students form trios to read Acts 16:6-10 and discuss these questions:

● **What was Paul waiting for?**

● **How did the Holy Spirit lead Paul?**

● **How was our game like the way the Holy Spirit led Paul? How was it different?**

● **Have circumstances ever led you away from something you were waiting for only to lead you to something better? Explain.**

Say: **Sometimes we want to rush into things we want. But often, the Holy Spirit makes us wait for what's best. We'll see how this happens in Paul's story.**

Hand each trio a sheet of paper and a pencil. Say: **In your trios,**

Leader tip

If you have more than twenty students, have four students run through the maze at a time. Start each student at a different corner.

read Acts 16:11-40. Then list all the good things that happened because Paul didn't go to the place he originally set out for. Then choose a way to share that information with the rest of the group. For example, you could choose to sing your list in operatic voices. You could build a pyramid and have the top person shout the answers. You could become a marching band using "instruments" like garbage cans and chairs and have your drum major cheer your answers. Whatever you choose to do, write your idea on the bottom of your sheet of paper.

After five minutes, say: **Oops! We're having a change of circumstance here! Hand your sheet of paper to another group and get another sheet from another group. You have three minutes to prepare the other group's lesson—what they learned and the way they intended to teach it.**

After three minutes, have each group present its new lesson. Then ask:

● **What was your reaction to trading lessons and having to wait longer to make a presentation?**

● **Did anything good come from the change and the waiting? Why or why not?**

● **How were the effects of this change like the effects of Paul's change in Acts 16? How were they different?**

● **How might the Holy Spirit change circumstances in your life to make you wait for what's best?**

Say: **When Paul tried to go to Bithynia, he was excited to share the good news of eternal life through Jesus Christ. He wanted to share that news with others so they could accept it. That was the passion of his heart. But the Holy Spirit knew better and made Paul wait for it. In the meantime, the Holy Spirit guided Paul to another place where Paul got to do what he wanted to do all along—share the gospel of Jesus Christ—with some incredible results! When we wait as guided by the Holy Spirit, we always end up in the best places with the best results.**

■ Wait Station (Reprise)

(5 to 10 minutes)

Supplies: Bibles, paper, pencils

Distribute Bibles, paper, and pencils to your students. Say: **We began this study with a time of silence, with you not knowing what to expect. We're going to close this study with another time of silence, and as we do, listen for the Holy Spirit. When we wait on the Holy Spirit, he leads us to what's best. So let's practice this now.**

Find a spot away from others. If you wish, close your eyes. You might choose to look up some verses. If you wish to do that, I recommend reading Romans 8:18-25 and Galatians 5:22-25. You might also want to write on your paper what you hear. Whatever you do, listen for the Holy Spirit to tell you about the part patience needs to play in your life.

Allow people five minutes of silence. Then encourage them to close their time of silence with a silent prayer.

Understanding Patience

When Jackie Robinson signed with the Brooklyn Dodgers in 1945, he became the first black baseball player to sign with a major league ball club. But one team signing him didn't mean that the rest of the league or the public would accept him. Jackie would have to fight a battle to gain recognition as a good baseball player in his own right, and the Dodger's general manager, Branch Rickey, knew that. When Rickey approached Robinson about playing for the Dodgers, he asked Robinson, "Do you have the guts not to fight back?" Rickey made Robinson promise that no matter what other ballplayers, fans, or the media threw his way, Robinson would take it all without ever striking back.

And Rickey's predictions were correct. Robinson had to endure great humiliation in his first years of baseball, both in the minor and major leagues. Civic leaders of various baseball towns required Robinson to leave their cities. Other city officials locked the gates of baseball parks and canceled games because he was on the team. After scoring in one game, a white police officer met Jackie at home plate and demanded that he leave. Pitchers threw at him, and other ballplayers insulted him. In some cities, Robinson wasn't allowed to stay at the same hotel as the rest of his team. Players threatened to strike instead of play against him.

But true to his promise, Robinson never said a word. When asked to leave cities and ballparks, he left. When pitchers threw at him, he hit the ground, then stood up, brushed himself off, and stepped into the batter's box again.

While he couldn't rush the pitcher or shout back at raging fans and city officials, Robinson fought the battle in his own way. Jackie fought back by playing excellent baseball. He showed everyone that he belonged in the major leagues on his own merit.

The situation was never easy, but eventually all of Robinson's patience paid off. Slowly people began to accept and even respect him. And in 1947, Jackie Robinson was named the National League Rookie of the Year. In addition, his perseverance paved the way for fellow black baseball players to enjoy America's national pastime.

(Story paraphrased from Hal Butler, "The Man Who Broke the Color Barrier," in *The Moral Compass*, edited by William J. Bennett, 1995)

Quiet Zone!

In a few moments, we'll begin our study.

While you wait, please sit quietly by yourself.

Don't talk or gesture to those around you.

Just spend the time preparing yourself for what's to come.

Thanks.

How Long...
h a n d o u t

1. How long did it take to create the Statue of Liberty (from the time the creator thought of the idea until the time President Grover Cleveland dedicated it)?
(a) 2 years (b) 6 years (c) 12 years (d) 14 years

2. How long does it take for an egg to hatch into a chick?
(a) 1 week (b) 2 weeks (c) 2½ weeks (d) 3 weeks

3. How long was it between the time Thomas Edison filed the papers for his first invention (an electric vote recorder) and his invention of the lamp?
(a) 5 years (b) 8 years (c) 10 years (d) 11 years

4. How long did it take 36 people in Annecy, France to make a bouquet 36 feet, 10 inches high and consisting of 9,299 flowers?
(a) 35 minutes (b) 335 minutes (c) 35 hours (d) 335 hours

5. What's the longest anyone (other than Jesus) has ever gone without food and water?
(a) 8 days (b) 18 days (c) 28 days (d) 32 days

6. What's the longest amount of time that a pair of twins has waited to be reunited?
(a) 75 days (b) 75 weeks (c) 75 months (d) 75 years

7. What's the longest one person has survived on a raft waiting for rescue?
(a) 6 weeks (b) 2 weeks (c) 3 months (d) 4½ months

8. How long did it take to complete Mount Rushmore?
(a) 14 years (b) 16 years (c) 20 years (d) 25 years

9. How long is the African elephant pregnant?
(a) 16 months (b) 18 months (c) 21 months (d) 24 months

10. How long did it take for the Bible to be written?
(a) 50 years (b) 160 years (c) 400 years (d) 1,600 years

11. What's one way each person in your trio has exhibited patience in his or her life?

↓Abram's Wait
h a n d o u t

Read Abram's story in Genesis 15:1-6; 16:1-12; and 21:1-21. Then discuss these questions:

- **What was Abram waiting for?**

- **How did he and Sarai exhibit impatience? Why do you think they did that?**

- **What were the results of Abram's impatience?**

- **What do you think would have happened if Abram and Sarai had waited for God to fulfill his plan?**

- **How was taking our patience test like Abram guessing when and how God would fulfill his plan? How was it different?**

- **Were the results of Abram and Sarai's impatience all bad? Why or why not?**

- **When have you been impatient in a situation? Would things have been different if you had waited a little bit longer? Why or why not?**

- **Why is it so hard to wait for things?**

- **What's something you're waiting for now that's hard to wait for? How could you be more patient in that situation?**

Out of the Gray

Applying the Bible to Daily Life

BIBLICAL POINT: The Bible is relevant to your life.
BIBLE BASIS: 1 Corinthians 8
TOPIC: Gray Areas of Scripture

If you ask people what the Bible is about, you can probably guess some typical responses:
"It's about stuff that happened a long time ago."
"It's a bunch of confusing rules."

Some people may understand that the Bible is God's Word for *today,* but they may not know how to apply it to their own lives and to the immediate circumstances they face. Where does the Bible talk about drugs? give guidelines for dating or choosing a career? address bills or employment or any of the myriad of pressures a young adult faces?

Young adults need to know that God's Word doesn't leave them to guess on their own. It offers guidelines and principles that can be applied to every situation they face. When students learn to search for these principles and apply them to their lives, they'll begin to see that the Bible is a powerful and relevant guide for life.

Before the study, gather the following supplies:
- Bibles,
- one "Resolved…" handout (p. 48) for each person,
- one "Acting on Principle" handout (p. 49) for each person,
- paper,
- pencils,
- newsprint,
- a marker, and
- tape.

out of the gray
● The Bible is relevant to your life.

■ Gray Areas

(10 to 15 minutes)
Supplies: Paper, pencils, newsprint, a marker, tape

Have students form groups of three; then give each trio a sheet of paper and a pencil. Ask each trio to choose a recorder and a reporter. Have the recorders draw vertical lines down their sheets of paper to create three columns of equal size. Have students write, "Definitely Wrong" at the top of the first column, "Gray Areas" at the top of the middle column, and "Definitely OK" at the top of the last column.

Say: **In the first column on your sheet of paper, have your recorder list at least three actions you would all definitely agree are wrong. In the last column, have your recorder list at least three actions that are definitely right. In the middle column, have your recorder list at least three actions that you think fall into the gray area.**

While the trios are working, use a marker and sheet of newsprint to create a large version of the three-column work sheets that students made. Tape the large work sheet to a wall.

Call everyone back together. Ask the reporters to read the actions their trios came up with. Have the recorders write the actions in the appropriate columns on the newsprint work sheet that you taped to the wall.

Ask:

● **Do you think the Bible effectively addresses the issues that the people face today? Why or why not?**

● **How would you make the decision whether to participate in something listed in the gray area?**

● **How can the Bible help you know what to do about a situation that isn't directly discussed in Scripture?**

● **Do you think the Bible is relevant to your life? Why or why not?**

Say: **The Bible doesn't directly address many of the issues we may face today. However, it does give principles and guidelines that we can apply to any situation. Let me show you what I mean.**

■ Biblical Debate

(25 to 35 minutes)

Supplies: Bibles, pencils, "Resolved..." handouts (p. 48)

Have students return to their trios. Ask the trio members who didn't act as recorders or reporters in the first activity to read aloud 1 Corinthians 8. Then have trios discuss these questions:

● **Why were the Christians in Corinth confused over the issue of eating meat that had been offered to idols?**

● **What principles did Paul give to help Christians decide how to act when they encountered the issue of eating meat that was offered to idols?**

● **Are these principles relevant to your life? If so, how? If not, why not?**

Have each trio choose one of the gray areas listed on the sheet of newsprint in the "Gray Areas" activity. Encourage each trio to take a different situation. Give each person a copy of the "Resolved..." handout and a pencil, and ask students to read the guidelines for their presentations. Answer any questions the students have. Then have each trio discuss its situation and prepare for its presentation.

Call everyone back together. Have the trios take turns presenting their situations according to the format in the handout. After each presentation, allow time for the other students to discuss and comment on the suggested application of 1 Corinthians 8. Prompt discussion with questions such as:

● **Do you think what the Bible says is relevant in this situation? Why or why not?**

● **Could there be a time when this action isn't OK? Explain.**

● **Could there be a time when this action is OK? Explain.**

● **What's the best way to handle this situation? Why do you think so?**

After all the trios have presented their situations, ask:

● **When would it be hard for you to give up your right to do something that *isn't* wrong?**

● **Have you ever done something that you believed was OK to do when someone else thought it was wrong? If so, what happened? How did you feel?**

● **Have you ever seen another Christian do something you thought was wrong? How did it affect you?**

● **Do you think the Bible is relevant to your life? Why or why not?**

Say: **At first glance, 1 Corinthians 8 may seem to be pretty irrelevant to today's culture. We probably don't spend much time worrying about whether the food we eat has been offered to idols. But if we look beyond the circumstances of this passage to the principles,**

Leader tip

If you don't have enough time to allow all the trios to stage their situations, you may want to stage two or more simultaneously in different areas of your meeting place.

Can Something Be Right for One Person and Wrong for Another?

In this age of situational ethics, it may be a little disconcerting to find that Paul suggests that what's right and wrong depends on...who you're with at the time!

Of course, some things are wrong no matter what: hatred, envy, and the attitudes and actions that flow from them. But some actions really aren't morally wrong in themselves; it's their impact on others that makes them harmful.

In Paul's culture, the meat offered for sale in the marketplace had sometimes first been offered to an idol. After the ritual ceremony had been performed, the meat could be sold.

Early Christians needed to know whether they were sinning by eating this meat. Were they in some way participating in the idol sacrifice if they bought the meat? What if they ate it without knowing where it came from? Where they still culpable?

Paul's direction to the people of Corinth was simple: Idols aren't real. They can't do anything to you, and neither can the meat sacrificed to them. There's no reason to worry about eating the meat.

But if you still feel guilty, don't eat it. You can't be healthy spiritually if you think you're doing something wrong. And if someone around you thinks it's wrong, then you shouldn't do it either. Make certain your action doesn't offend that person or tempt him or her to act against his or her conscience.

The importance isn't in what you eat, but in whether you are trying to nurture your own spiritual growth and that of those around you.

To supplement the "Acting on Principle" handout, you can provide other resources to help students find appropriate Scripture passages for their gray areas:

● **Concordances** can be helpful if a person has a particular passage in mind but doesn't know where to find it. Concordances are of limited use in looking up certain topics because many of the gray areas students wonder about will likely relate to contemporary issues that are not specifically mentioned—for example, drug use, music or movie choices, or employment questions.

● Many **study Bibles** have lists that point readers to specific passages. *The Student Bible* (NIV), for example, contains a "Subject Guide" that lists passages dealing with subjects of interest including abortion, homosexuality, popularity, and suicide. *The Quest Study Bible* (NIV) provides cultural background and in-depth explanations for difficult questions.

we'll find that God has given an excellent example to help us determine how to use the freedom he has given us. This is an issue every Christian must deal with. As we learn to look beyond the surface and search for the principles in God's Word, we find that the Bible is relevant to our lives.

■ Acting on Principle

(10 to 15 minutes)

Supplies: Bibles, pencils, "Acting on Principle" handouts (p. 49)

Have people return to their trios. Then say: **Let each person in your group share a gray-area issue that he or she struggles with. Then pray for the person on your right. Ask God to help that person find and apply God's principles to his or her gray area.**

Distribute pencils and a photocopy of "Acting on Principle" handout to each person. Then say: **In your trios, use this handout to brainstorm about biblical principles that address a gray area you sometimes struggle with. Discuss how you can apply those principles to your situation. Be sure to circle or jot down the principles that apply to your own gray area.**

When students finish, ask:

● **Were you able to find biblical principles that addressed your gray area?**

● **What's the best way to deal with your gray area?**

● **Are there any areas of life that the Bible doesn't help us deal with? Explain.**

Say: **It isn't always easy to act on the principles you uncover. But you've probably already had some practice—maybe without even realizing it. Look at the principles the other people in your trio circled or jotted down on their sheets. Take a minute to recall ways you've seen them act on those principles in the past. Then take turns telling about the principles you've already seen at work in each other's lives.**

Truth or Consequences

People don't always recognize the consequences of their actions. Disobedience, even to God's commands, may seem immaterial. Young people may argue that since God will forgive them, it's not really a big deal if they make the wrong choice—especially if they aren't hurting anyone else. But disobeying God's laws often hurts people—not necessarily as a punishment, but as a natural consequence. For example,

● sex outside of marriage can result in a damaged reputation, loss of self-respect, sexually transmitted disease, and unwanted pregnancy.

● drunkenness can lead to addiction, health problems, failed relationships, lost jobs, and fatal automobile accidents.

● stealing can lead to a criminal record and broken trust. It can blunt the thief's conscience, lead to other crimes, or saddle him or her with crippling guilt.

● gossip ruins friendships, gives the "gossip" the reputation of being two-faced, and leaves the victim wondering what others are saying when he or she isn't nearby.

"We know that we all possess knowledge. Knowledge puffs up, but love builds up. The man who thinks he knows something does not yet know as he ought to know. But the man who loves God is known by God."

—1 Corinthians 8:1b-3

Resolved...
handout

As a trio, choose one of the gray-area situations listed earlier, and discuss it. Each of you should choose one of the three roles explained below. If more than three people are in your group, two people can team up for a role. Plan how you'll present your gray-area situation for the "Set the Stage" part of this activity. Then take a few minutes alone to prepare your arguments and responses. Follow this format to present your gray-area situation:

The Format

1. Set the Stage

- You are all actors. Show everyone what decision the person must make by acting out an event that leads the person to decide if he or she will participate in your gray-area activity. Stop the skit just before the person must make the choice.

- Try to present circumstances in which the choice is not obvious.

2. Convince the Person

- After you have stopped the skit, pause for a few seconds. The persuader and dissuader should stand on opposite sides of the person.

- The persuader has one minute to convince the person *to* participate in the activity. The person and the dissuader may not talk.

- The dissuader has one minute to convince the person *not to* participate in the activity. The person and the persuader may not talk.

- After both have presented their arguments, the person may question them. Then they may debate each other's arguments.

3. The Decision

- After the persuader and the dissuader have debated, the person must choose whether or not to participate in the activity. The person must also explain his or her choice.

The Roles

4. The Person

- During "Set the Stage," act as the one who must decide whether or not to participate in the gray area. Play the part of someone who isn't certain what to do.

- During "Convince the Person," listen to what the others say, and then ask questions. Address the holes in their arguments.

- During "The Decision," make a choice and then explain your choice. Use 1 Corinthians 8 as your guide, and explain to the group how the passage applies to your gray area.

5. The Persuader

- During "Set the Stage," help demonstrate the situation the person is facing.

- During "Convince the Person," act as the conscience of the person. Try to use the Bible, logic, and emotions to convince the person to participate in the gray area. After the person asks questions, debate the weaknesses you saw in the dissuader's argument.

6. The Dissuader

- During "Set the Stage," help demonstrate the situation the person is facing.

- During "Convince the Person," act as the conscience of the person. Use the Bible, logic, and emotions to convince the person not to participate in the gray area. After the person asks questions, debate the weaknesses you saw in the persuader's argument.

Acting on Principle

handout

The Bible doesn't always directly address the situations we find ourselves in. But the principles in the Bible are always relevant to our lives.

Here are some general biblical principles. Read them, look up the passages that seem most appropriate, and discuss in your trio how one or more of these principles apply to the specific situation you are facing. Circle or jot down the principles that seem most relevant to your own personal gray-area situation.

Principle	Where to Find It
If it brings blessings, do it.	Deuteronomy 30:19-20
If it points others to God, do it.	Matthew 5:13-16
If it hurts someone else in any way, don't do it.	Matthew 7:12
If it's illegal, don't do it.	Romans 13:1-5
If God doesn't honor it, don't do it.	1 Corinthians 6:12-20
If it goes against your parents' wishes, don't do it.	Ephesians 6:1-3
If it puts others first, do it.	Philippians 2:1-11
If it honors Jesus Christ, do it.	Colossians 3:17

When God Seems Silent

BIBLICAL POINT: God always answers your prayers.

BIBLE BASIS: Matthew 26:36-46 and 2 Corinthians 12:7-10

TOPIC: Prayer

"**I** prayed...nothing happened."

How many times have you heard that lament from your students—or thought it yourself? And yet, even after weeks or months of seeking God, people still don't stop praying and hoping God will hear them, hoping he will answer, hoping they might stumble upon the secret to this mysterious link with God we call prayer.

Confusion...rejection...relief...Prayer can evoke a gamut of emotions and responses. This study focuses on people's honest comments about prayer to help your group members confront their own doubts about prayer. They'll examine several views of prayer and two experiences of seemingly unanswered prayer in the Bible.

Through this examination, group members will be challenged to pursue an intimate prayer relationship with an infinite, caring God—a God who always hears their cries and always answers.

Before the study, designate an area near your meeting room (or in an out-of-the-way corner of your meeting room) as a "praying spot." Then, on a sheet of paper, list your entire study time in five-minute intervals. After each time interval, draw a blank line to list a person's name. For example, if your study starts at 7 p.m., your list should begin like this:

7:00 _____

7:05 _____

7:10 _____

Also photocopy and cut apart the quotes in the "Views of Prayer" handout (p. 57). Tape the quotes on walls all over your meeting room. (It's OK to post the same quote in more than one place.)

You'll also need

● Bibles,

● paper,

● a clock,

● pencils,

● tape,

● index cards, and

● a calendar.

when God seems silent

● God always answers your prayers.

51

■ Prayer Shift

(up to 5 minutes)

Supplies: Paper, a clock, a pencil

As students arrive, solicit volunteers willing to spend a five-minute shift during the study talking to God in the designated praying spot. If necessary to fill up the study time, allow students to sign up for more than one five-minute shift. Or if you have more students than shifts, you might consider allowing more than one student to sign up for the same shift. Write down each volunteer's name next to his or her shift; then instruct volunteers to keep an eye on the clock and quietly excuse themselves at the appropriate times.

■ Views of Prayer

(15 to 20 minutes)

Supplies: Quotes from "Views of Prayer" handout (p. 57)

Have everyone form a circle in the middle of the room; then ask everyone to face away from the center of the circle. Say: **Today we're going to examine the idea of prayer, and I'd like to hear your views about this topic. Posted all around the room are quotes expressing a variety of perspectives on prayer. You've got three minutes to examine the quotes and carry back to this circle the quote that most expresses the way you feel about prayer. Ready? Go.**

After everyone has chosen a quote, have people gather around you and then toss their chosen quotes into a pile. One by one, select a quote from the pile, read it aloud; then say: **If you agree with this quote, move to my left. If you disagree, move to my right.**

Things to Pray About

● Think of descriptive words about God. Pray, "God, you are…" and complete the sentence with the descriptive words.

● Think of all the ways you can see God at work today—in the sunrise, in a friend's encouragement, or in a special Bible verse, for example. Then complete this sentence as you pray: "God, I saw you today in…"

● Think of three things you did—or didn't do—over the past week that you know God wouldn't approve of. Then describe those things to God, and ask him to forgive those mistakes.

● Think of five good things about your life. Then give God thanks for those things.

● Pray for each person in the study by name, and ask God to show kindness and love to each person in some tangible way.

● Ask God to guide the study's leader and all the participants during this meeting so you can all have a great time of discovery together.

After you read each quote, wait for students to respond, and then ask a few people from each group to explain their choices.

Read as many quotes as time allows. Then have everyone find a partner and sit down to discuss these questions:

● **Why do you think there are so many different opinions about prayer?**

● **Have you ever felt that prayer might be a waste of time? Explain.**

● **Why do you suppose virtually all major religions teach about prayer or something similar, such as meditation?**

● **When has prayer made a difference in your life?**

● **What's one question you have about prayer? How do you think you might find an answer to that question?**

● **How would you describe prayer to someone who had never heard of it before? What might you compare it to?**

● **Why do you think some prayers seem to go unanswered?**

Ask a few volunteers to report about their discussions to the rest of the study. Then say: **I believe God always answers our prayers, but even the Bible tells of times when it seemed as if God didn't respond to prayers. Let's look into this more.**

■ Unanswered Prayer?

(10 to 15 minutes)
Supplies: Bibles

Have people form foursomes; then say: **In a moment, we're going to read about two people in the Bible whose prayers seemed to go unanswered. But to make this reading a bit challenging, let's try reading the passages from a distance.**

Have each group open a Bible to Matthew 26:36-46, prop the open Bible against a wall, and then step back about seven or eight feet. Tell group members to work as a team to read the passage from that distance—without stepping forward. If group members need to turn a page to read the whole passage, have them select a "designated flipper" to move forward, flip the page, and then return to the foursome.

Have foursomes repeat the process for 2 Corinthians 12:7-10. When groups finish each passage, have them retrieve their Bibles to see how accurately they were able to read the passage. Then have foursomes discuss these questions:

● **How did trying to read the passages from a distance make you feel?**

● **How is that like trying to pray when God seems silent or far away?**

Ask for a volunteer to read aloud each passage again for the whole group. Then have foursomes continue their discussions with these questions:

● **What are your thoughts about prayer after hearing about the experiences of Jesus and Paul in these two passages?**

If all students gather on one side in response to a quote, ask for a few volunteers to play the "devil's advocate" and defend the opposite viewpoint.

Don't forget to quietly check every once in a while to make sure at least one person is at the praying spot at all times.

Biblical Background

In Matthew 26:36-46, Jesus expresses great sorrow over a "cup" and prays for God to deliver him from it. Some theologians believe that "cup" may refer back to an Old Testament "cup of the Lord's wrath" in Isaiah 51:17-23. In that passage, the prophet describes God's punishment as a cup filled with wrath to be poured out on people because of their sin. Because Jesus would take on the whole world's sin through the cross, he would then become the sole object of God's cup of wrath as well.

God answered Jesus' prayer for deliverance from this cup—and that answer was no.

The result? Forgiveness and new life for millions who would trust in Jesus' death and resurrection for salvation.

Biblical Background

In 2 Corinthians 12:7-10, Paul refers to a "thorn in my flesh." Scholars often disagree about what that "thorn" might have been. Some say it was simply temptation. Others think it might have been things such as opposition to his faith, bad vision, headaches, epilepsy, malaria, or a speech impediment. But regardless of what the problem was, it's important to note that God did answer Paul's prayer. Paul wanted healing; God's answer was grace in weakness instead.

● **How were Jesus and Paul able to remain strong in their faith despite these seemingly unanswered prayers?**
● **Do you think Jesus or Paul would agree with the statement: "God always answers your prayers"? Why or why not?**
● **Do you think the degree of intimacy in Jesus' and Paul's relationships with God helped them handle these "unanswered prayers"?**
● **Do you think God answered Jesus' and Paul's prayers? Explain.**
● **What would it take for you to believe that God always answers your prayers? Explain.**

■ Questions on Prayer

(10 to 15 minutes)

Supplies: Bibles, index cards, pencils

Still in their foursomes, have people assign group members the following roles: a clerk who records the group's thoughts on an index card, a leader who coordinates the group discussion, a reporter who reports the group's answers to everyone else, and a director who includes all group members in the discussion.

Give an index card and a pencil to each clerk. Say: **You've read about two biblical prayer experiences. Now imagine you could ask Jesus or Paul any question at all about *your* experiences with prayer. What's the one question your group would ask?**

Give foursomes two minutes to discuss their ideas. When each foursome has written a question on an index card, have foursomes trade cards with each other. Then give foursomes about three minutes to answer the questions as if they were Jesus or Paul.

When everyone is ready, have foursomes take turns reading the questions and sharing their answers with the study. Then gather everyone in a circle once more, this time facing inward. Ask:

● **If God always answers your prayers—even if God's answers aren't what you expect or hope for—then how will that affect your attitudes and actions this week?**

Say: **We often use prayer to let God know about our needs, but prayers don't always have to be requests. In fact, I'd like to take a minute right now to give thanks to God.**

Think for a moment about one or two words that describe a positive contribution the person on your right has made to our meeting time today. For example, you might choose "enthusiasm" because the person to your right always participated enthusiastically. Or you might choose "insightful" because that person put a lot of thought into his or her answers during our discussions.

Pause while students think of their words. Then say: **I'm going to begin a sentence to start our prayer. Then I'd like us to go around the circle and take turns saying our chosen words to complete the sentence and the prayer.**

When everyone is ready, pray: **Lord, thank you so much for using the people in this circle to contribute the following things to this group...** Add a positive word or two about the person to your right. After everyone has had a turn, close the prayer.

Leader tip

If a foursome struggles with trying to figure out how Jesus or Paul might respond to a question, encourage group members to look up additional Scriptures that describe these men's characters in more detail. Here are some examples:
● Jesus—Matthew 6:5-15, 25-34; and 7:7-11.
● Paul—Romans 8:26-28; Ephesians 6:18-20; Philippians 4:6-7; and 1 Thessalonians 5:16-22.
You may even want to write a list of these Scriptures on newsprint and tape it to a wall for foursomes to use.

■ Prayer Challenge Campaign

(5 to 10 minutes)

Supplies: Paper, pencils, a calendar

Say: **We've raised a lot of questions about prayer today, but the most basic question we've asked is this: Does God always answer prayer? I propose we do a little experiment to find out.**

Encourage students to organize a Prayer Challenge Campaign. Tell them that the campaign's goal is simply to get as many people as they can to commit to praying the following prayer at least once a day for seven days: "Lord, show me this week whether prayer is worthwhile."

Spend the rest of your study time planning the campaign's details. On the calendar, designate a week within the next month to be the prayer week; then plan strategies to encourage people to sign up for the campaign.

For example, group members might make fliers to place around the church or at work or school, place an ad in a local newspaper, or simply ask ten people to participate.

Set a date for a follow-up meeting to discuss the experience after the week of prayer. Invite everyone who participated to come and report the results of their prayer experiments. Use that meeting to help group members discover how God might have answered their prayers and to examine why or why not prayers may seem to have gone unanswered for some.

Americans and Prayer

● According to a Gallup survey, nine of ten Americans pray. In fact, 75 percent of Americans say they pray every day.

● A full 95 percent of Americans report they've experienced answers to prayer.

● Among people born from 1965 to 1983, 64 percent rate "having a close relationship with God" as a very desirable life condition.

● Of people born between 1965 and 1983, 62 percent believe that "God hears all people's prayers and has the power to answer those prayers."

● Ironically, among *churchgoing* people born between 1965 and 1983, 40 percent say they've never felt God's presence at any time in their lives.

Views of Prayer
handout

Photocopy and cut apart the quotes on this page to use in the "Views of Prayer" activity.

--- ✂

"I don't think God really cares what God you pray to as long as you've said your prayers."

—KathG, from America Online

--- ✂

"Be clear minded and self-controlled so that you can pray."

—1 Peter 4:7b

--- ✂

"Any thoughts on prayer? Yeah. It's dumb."

—Phlanax, from America Online

--- ✂

"I'm curious what makes people [pray]. It seems pointless to me."

—Cuillin 2, from America Online

--- ✂

"Prayer is a very powerful thing...it works for me."

—Bridget2, from America Online

--- ✂

"I think whether [prayer] works or not depends on the person praying. If you think it works, it probably will."

—JENNYN3010, from America Online

--- ✂

"Prayer = brownie points with God."

—Dave 911, from America Online

--- ✂

"Is any one of you in trouble? He should pray...The prayer of a righteous man is powerful and effective."

—James 5:13a, 16b

--- ✂

"I believe in God, but I don't think God answers every prayer. One in 10,000 maybe."

—Brenke, from America Online

--- ✂

Looking In
looking in

Facing the Real Enemy

Dealing With Spiritual Forces in Your Life

BIBLICAL POINT: Spiritual forces are at work in your life.

BIBLE BASIS: Colossians 2:1-15

TOPIC: Spiritual Warfare

introduction

Urban blight. It's ugly. It's discouraging. It marks the slow death of a neighborhood. Spiritual blight is even uglier.

Spiritual forces are real and are at work in your group members' lives. Satan wants to blight their spiritual growth. Sometimes the decay is slow—a crumbling of ethical standards here, a crack in assurance there. Neglect is one of Satan's most potent weapons. And when people neglect their spiritual lives, they go downhill.

But Satan isn't the only spiritual force in town. God wrote the master plan on renewal. And God has given us tools for constructing healthy, empowered spiritual lives.

In this study, students will form "construction crews" for a hands-on exploration of Colossians 2:1–15. By building objects that represent positive tools for spiritual growth, students will discover constructive ways God helps them overcome destructive forces in their spiritual lives.

Before the study, read through the study, beginning with the "Construction Site" handouts (pp. 66-67), to get a clear idea of how the study will flow.

Write each of the following quotes from actual young people on half a sheet of paper. Write the quotes in a "graffiti" style, and use block-style capital letters. Then use a marker to draw a border around each quote so it looks like a brick.

● "Sometimes I don't feel like a Christian. It's like I'm being pulled in two directions."

—Val

● "It's like I'd have arguments in my head about what I believe. Constantly I'd be asking myself which one is God's voice and which one is Satan's voice."

—Matt

facing the real enemy

● Spiritual forces are at work in your life.

● "When I read the Bible, I have all these doubts. I mean, am I really supposed to believe that a man could live inside a whale?"

—Jennifer

● "Any time you're tempted to do something wrong, I think that's spiritual warfare."

—Mike

Make enough "bricks" so that every student can have at least one. (You may write each quote more than once.) Tape the bricks at different spots along three walls in your room, but leave one wall blank for the "Graffiti Wall" activity. You'll also need

● Bibles,
● masking tape,
● four "Construction Site" handouts (pp. 66-67),
● assorted supplies as described in the "Christians Under Construction" activity (p. 63), and
● pushpins or tacks.

Leader tip ▼

Throughout this study, you or the various construction crews will be reading some Bible verses more than once. People learn through repetition, and group members may get fresh insight when they hear the same verse in a slightly different context. For this reason, make sure people go back to the Scripture and read the passage each time they're asked to.

■ Graffiti Wall

(5 to 10 minutes)

Supplies: Quotes created before the study, masking tape

As students arrive, have them roam the room and read the quotes. Have them choose quotes they identify with (they can choose more than one) and tape the "bricks" to the blank wall to "build" a brick wall.

When everyone has finished, read aloud the various quotes, inviting people to comment on them. Point out that some quotes describe feeling, some describe thought, and some describe action.

Then say: **When you see walls in a neighborhood that are covered with graffiti, you know that negative forces are at work in that community. When you experience the situations that the "graffiti" on our "wall" describes, you know that negative forces are at work in your spiritual life. Satan would like to build a wall between you and God. Let's explore how we can construct some tools to dismantle that wall.**

■ Christians Under Construction

(20 to 25 minutes)

Supplies: Bibles, "Construction Site" handouts (pp. 66-67), assorted supplies as described below.

Have people form four "construction crews," and send each crew to one of the sites described below.

Each construction site has two options. For each site, choose the option that best fits your needs, or use both. You'll need to provide the following supplies:

Construction Site 1: Lifeline—Bibles, bathroom tissue, and pens.

Construction Site 2: Treasure Chest—Bibles, index cards, pens, a box with a lid (such as a shoe box), and materials for making a treasure chest (such as markers, paper, aluminum foil, tape, and scissors).

For option 2 only, you'll also need tape and one foil-wrapped chocolate coin for each person in the study.

Construction Site 3: Growth Lab—Bibles and one small, clear-plastic cup for each member of the study.

For option 1 only, you'll also need potting soil, large spoons, seeds, and a watering can filled with water.

For option 2 only, you'll also need one spoon for each member of the study, a mixing bowl, a measuring cup, a plastic bag, a rolling pin, a whisk, and ingredients for "Dirt Cups" from the "Growth Lab" portion (p. 67) of the "Construction Site" handout.

Construction Site 4: Cross—Bibles and markers.

For option 1 only, you'll also need one six-foot two-by-four, one four-foot two-by-four, hammers, and nails.

For option 2 only, you'll also need glue and two craft sticks for each person in the study.

Give each crew the appropriate section of the "Construction Site" handout, and have crews work from their handouts. Circulate from crew to crew as they work.

■ On-Site Tour

(5 to 10 minutes)
Supplies: None needed

When the crews have finished their construction projects and have discussed the questions on their handouts, call everyone back together. Say: **Spiritual forces are at work in your life. Some of those forces try to put up a wall between you and God. But God is a Spirit, too, and he is the most powerful force. Let's tour the construction sites to see what kind of tools we can build—with God's help—that will tear down the wall between us and God.**

Lead the group through the four sites, stopping to do the following activities.

Construction Site 1: Lifeline—Have a crew member read aloud Colossians 2:1-2. Have the reporter share the crew's responses to the questions on the handout.

For option 1 only, have each person tear off an end of the lifeline and read aloud the suggestion written on it. Encourage people to act on the ideas at home during the week.

For option 2 only, have each person tear off an end of the lifeline, read aloud the affirmation, and present it to the person whose name is on it.

Leader tip ▼

The construction sites work best with a minimum of two students and a maximum of eight. If you have fewer than eight people, assign each construction crew more than one site. If you have more than thirty-two people, have part of each construction crew do option 1 and another part do option 2 for each site.

Leader tip ▼

In option 2 of the "Growth Lab" activity, the recipe for dirt cups works best if you can refrigerate the snack until the end of the meeting. If a cool spot isn't available, the crew can still make the snack; it will just be a little messier to eat!

Biblical Background

One construction crew will be asked to find contrasts listed in Colossians 2:8-14. If students have trouble with this assignment, help them out with the following clues:

● Hollow and deceptive philosophy (verse 8) vs. fullness in Christ (verse 10).

● Human tradition and basic principles of the world (verse 8) vs. Christ, who is head over every power and authority (verse 10).

● The sinful nature (verse 11) vs. the power of God (verse 12).

● Buried vs. raised (verse 12).

● Dead in sins vs. alive with Christ (verse 13).

Give students the first half of each contrast, and challenge them to find its opposite in the passage. Also note that the wording here is based on the New International Version of the Bible; other translations may use different words.

Construction Site 2: Treasure Chest—Have a crew member read aloud Colossians 2:2-5. Have the reporter share the crew's responses to the questions on the handout.

For option 1 only, have crew members read aloud the counterfeit and true sides of their index cards.

For option 2 only, have crew members hand out the chocolate coins. Encourage people to take the coins home and look up the attached references this week.

Construction Site 3: Growth Lab—Have crew members present the object lesson they've prepared. (The Scripture is incorporated in the object lesson.)

For option 2 only, you can let people eat their dirt cups now or save them until the end of the meeting.

Construction Site 4: Cross—Have a crew member read aloud Colossians 2:8-14. Have the reporter share the crew's response to the question on the handout.

For option 1 only, have crew members read the contrasts on the big cross.

For option 2 only, have crew members read the contrasts on the small crosses. Have crew members hand out the small crosses. Encourage people to take the crosses home and hang them somewhere noticeable—such as on their rearview mirrors.

■ Cleanup

(10 to 15 minutes)

Supplies: Pushpins or tacks, cross (or crosses) from the "Christians Under Construction" activity

Read aloud Colossians 2:13-15. Say: **Spiritual forces are real and at work in your life. But God has stripped the spiritual rulers and authorities of their power. Now the spiritual power in your life is the power of the Cross. Go over to the graffiti wall, and strip down the bricks. Make sure everyone has at least one brick, and make sure every brick comes down. Then bring your bricks and form a circle.**

If students did option 1 for construction site 4, lay the cross on the floor in the center of the room. If students did option 2 for construction site 4, have the students lay the crosses on the floor in the shape of one large cross. Place a box of pushpins or tacks beside the cross or crosses.

When people have formed a circle, read Colossians 2:13-14 again. Say: **Think about a sin that has overpowered you. God has taken that sin and nailed it to the cross. When you're ready, pin your brick to our cross to represent what God has already done with the sins in your life. As you pin your brick to the cross, say a silent prayer to God.**

■ Topping Off

(up to 5 minutes)

Supplies: None needed

Say: **When construction workers reach the high point of their building, they sometimes celebrate by putting a Christmas tree on top of the building. And although Christ's cross looks—from a human perspective—like the low point of his life, it is actually the high point in the spiritual battle.**

Read aloud Colossians 2:15 again. Then gather everyone close to the cross. As people stand around the cross, raise up Christ's name in praise, either with prayers or a song.

Construction Site
h a n d o u t

Construction Site 1: Lifeline
(Option 1)

1. Read Colossians 2:1-2.

2. Tear off a strip of bathroom tissue at least twenty squares long for each person in the room.

3. As a crew, discuss examples of how to "encourage in heart and unite in love" (verse 2). These should be practical things you could do this week, such as "Write an encouraging note to someone in this group." As a crew member calls out an idea, have someone write it at the end of one strip of bathroom tissue so that you have a different idea on an end of each strip. If you run out of ideas, you can use your best ideas more than once.

4. Braid or twist all the strips together to form a "lifeline." Leave the last ends (with the writing) hanging loose at one end of the lifeline.

5. Discuss these questions, and appoint a reporter to share your conclusions with the other construction crews:
● How are Christians who are "united in love" like the lifeline you made?
● How can "unity in love" help you experience God's power to overcome the evil spiritual forces at work in your life?

(Option 2)

Follow the directions for option 1, but for the third step, write the name of each person in the room on the end of a strip of bathroom tissue and an example of how that person has demonstrated love in the group. For example, someone might write, "Brent always listens and cares about others." Don't forget to do steps 4 and 5!

Construction Site 2: Treasure Chest
(Option 1)

1. Read Colossians 2:2-5.

2. Using the materials provided, spend no more than ten minutes creating a treasure chest.

3. Create a treasure by writing out the counterfeit arguments below onto separate index cards and then writing a Christlike response on the back of each card.
● Cheating is no big deal. It doesn't hurt anybody, and everybody else does it.
● If God were really loving and all-powerful, he'd stop the suffering in the world.
● Sex outside of marriage is OK if you really love the person.
● To be a Christian, you have to check your brain at the door.
● You can be a healthy, growing Christian without ever interacting with other Christians.

4. Discuss these questions, and appoint a reporter to share your conclusions with the other construction crews:
● What does it mean to you to have the "riches" and "treasures" that verses 2 and 3 talk about?
● How does the treasure you created help you understand how God's power can overcome the evil spiritual forces at work in your life?

(Option 2)

Follow the directions for option 1, but for the third step, write a reference to a favorite or meaningful Scripture plus a comment of your own, and tape it to one of the chocolate coins. Make enough so each person can take one home. (You can use the same passage more than once.) Don't forget to do step 4!

Construction Site 3: Growth Lab
(Option 1)

1. Read Colossians 2:6-8.

2. As a crew, use the materials provided to develop an object lesson for the rest of the group. Everyone on your crew must be involved. Follow this outline, or create your own:

Construction Site
(continued)
h a n d o u t

a. Have one or more crew members read aloud Colossians 2:8. Then hand out the plastic cups to everyone, and share how your crew members completed these sentences:
- "Hollow" or "deceptive" philosophies are like an empty cup because...
- Some "hollow" philosophies that threaten us spiritually are...
- Hollow philosophies draw us away from God by...

b. Have someone read aloud Colossians 2:6-7a. Then have all the crew members fill the cups with dirt while one or more members share how they completed this sentence:
- Good soil can remind us of the faith we've been taught because...

c. Have all the crew members hand out seeds, and instruct everyone to plant the seeds while one or more crew members share how they completed this sentence:
- Some ways we can keep our roots deep in Christ are...

d. Have someone read aloud Colossians 2:7b. Then pass around a watering can, and give these instructions:
- When the watering can comes to you, water your seed, and name one thing you're thankful for.

e. Have one or more crew members tell how they completed this sentence:
- Being thankful helps us experience God's power and overcome evil spiritual forces at work in our lives because...

(Option 2)

Follow the directions in option 1 but instead of using real dirt and seeds, mix up the recipe below, and help the other crews assemble their own "dirt cups" for snacks. At each step, be sure to share the sentence completions. Use the jelly beans to replace the seeds. Instead of using a watering can and water, have people make their cups "overflow" by putting spoons in and sharing something they're thankful for.

Dirt Cups

This recipe makes 8 to 10 cups. Double as needed.

16 ounces chocolate sandwich cookies

2 cups cold milk

1 package chocolate instant pudding (the 4-serving size)

8 ounces whipped topping

8-10 clear plastic cups

jelly beans

With a rolling pin, crush the cookies in a plastic bag. Pour milk into a large bowl. Add pudding mix. Beat with whisk 1 to 2 minutes. Let stand 5 minutes. Stir in whipped topping and half of the crushed cookies. Place 1 tablespoon of crushed cookies in each cup. Fill cups 3/4 full with pudding. Top with remaining crushed cookies. Refrigerate until ready to serve.

Construction Site 4: Cross

(Option 1)

1. Read Colossians 2:8-14.

2. Using the materials provided, build a cross.

3. As a group, find as many contrasts as you can in verses 8 through 14—for example, "hollow and deceptive philosophy" (verse 8) vs. "fullness in Christ" (verse 10). Write each contrast on the cross, and make sure each crew member writes something.

4. Discuss this question, and appoint a reporter to share your conclusions with the other construction crews:
- What do these contrasts have to do with the spiritual forces at work in your life?

(Option 2)

Follow the directions for option 1, but for the second step, make a small cross for each person in the room. For the third step, write one contrast on each small cross. Don't forget to do step 4!

Setting a Course for Life

Developing Moral Character in Your Life

BIBLICAL POINT: God wants you to have moral character.

BIBLE BASIS: Deuteronomy 5:6-21 and Hebrews 12:1-2

TOPIC: Moral Character

When you get right down to it, ministry is all about destiny...purpose...helping people set a straight course for their lives. We want people to fix their spiritual sextants firmly on the Morning Star, Jesus Christ, and follow him to the end of the earth and back, without deviation or doubt.

But it's a stormy world out there. The waves can look like tsunamis. And the stars can be obscured by ominous clouds. What do we do to help students stay true to the course of life in Christ when threatening pressures assail them from every side?

Give them an inner compass to guide them through the storm. We call it "moral character." And this study shows people how to build it.

Before the study, gather the following supplies:
- Bibles,
- paper,
- pencils,
- cardboard,
- straws,
- thread or yarn,
- markers,
- tape,
- scissors,
- assorted craft items as described in the "Ships Ahoy" activity, (p. 71)
- newsprint, and
- one "My Life Code" handout (p. 75) for each person.

setting a course for life
- God wants you to have moral character.

69

Leader tip

Some of the information in this study has been adapted from the book *The Seven Habits of Highly Effective People* by Stephen R. Covey (Simon & Schuster). If you haven't read this book, consider reading it before the study. Both you and your group members will benefit from the additional insight Covey provides concerning personal mission statements or "life codes."

■ Begin With the End

(up to 5 minutes)

Supplies: Paper, pencils

As people arrive, have them form groups of four. Give each group paper and pencils. Once everyone has arrived, say: **We've had a great study today! I'm so glad each of you has had the opportunity to think about who you really want to be in life. Now I want you to work with your group to create a personal mission statement for each person in your group. Remember, the statement should take into account all the roles you play in life. When everyone is finished, we'll close with prayer. OK, you can get started.**

Wait about a minute while students try to follow your instructions. Then stop the activity, and ask people to discuss these questions in their groups:

● **Is anything bothering you about this activity? If so, what?**

● **Do you feel ready to do the closing activity for this study? Why or why not?**

● **How does that feeling compare to feeling unprepared to move into the future?**

● **Do you think it's important to have a sense of purpose in life? Why or why not?**

Call groups together, and say: **I decided to "begin with the end" today to illustrate why it's important to think about the kind of person you really want to be; after all, the decisions you make today shape your destiny—the future of your life's story.**

Understanding Your Students

Create a personal life code? You must be kidding! These students don't even know what they want to do tomorrow. How can I expect them to decide what they're going to be like for the rest of their lives?

Young adults are exploring, finding their own paths as separate from their parents. Although some young adults may feel they're well on their way to becoming the people they want to be, many of your students are still playing with different roles, trying to get a picture of their possible future selves.

That's where creating a personal life code can really help. In his book *The Seven Habits of Highly Effective People*, Stephen R. Covey writes, "There are principles that govern human effectiveness—natural laws in the human dimension that are just as real, just as unchanging and unarguably 'there' as laws such as gravity are in the physical dimension."

Creating a personal life code can help young adults recognize the spiritual principles or "laws" that lead to true success in life. And even if your students don't follow their codes perfectly, just having created it can help build within your students a sense of purpose and direction.

God wants your life to have moral character. And living by a personal "code" builds that character and firmly sets the course of your life so that things like stress and personal conflicts won't ever keep you from reaching your potential in Christ.

Today we're going to help each other develop personal codes to live by so that we can discover the power moral character brings to our lives.

■ Ships Ahoy

(10 to 15 minutes)

Supplies: Paper, cardboard, straws, thread or yarn, markers, tape, scissors, assorted craft items

Say: **To start our odyssey toward creating a personal life code, we're going to create personalized sailboats to help us rediscover just what kind of people we are.**

Set out paper, cardboard, straws, thread or yarn, markers, tape, scissors, and as many other assorted craft items as you can find, such as cloth scraps, pipe cleaners, craft sticks, toothpicks, rubber bands, paper clips, and pencils. Have people use the supplies to design and create their own sailboats. Tell people that they don't have to make anything elaborate—just something that definitely has sails. Encourage students to work together as they like, but remind them that each person needs to have his or her own sailboat.

■ Trade Winds

(up to 5 minutes)

Supplies: Sailboats

When everyone has completed a sailboat, have students form pairs and explain to their partners at least three ways their sailboats represent them.

Then have partners trade sailboats. Gather everyone together in a circle, and say: **God wants us to have moral character. But that doesn't mean we'll all be alike. Just look at the variety of sailboats we have! Each of us is unique and special to God. Having character means discovering who God made you to be and then living that out to the best of your ability.**

Now let's go around the circle, and each of you tell one unique quality about the boat you're holding. Then tell how that unique quality makes your partner special.

Starting with the person on your right, go around the circle and allow people to share. Then have everyone return the sailboat to its owner. Have people set their boats on the floor and join hands for prayer.

Leader tip ▼

You might consider building your own sailboat before the study to show everyone as an example. Or if you have access to pictures of sailboats (in calendars, magazines, or books), bring them in for people to look at.

Leader tip ▼

It's better if people don't spend too much time fussing over the details of their sailboats. The boats will be used later as tools for creating personal life codes and may be written on or damaged in the process.

Pray: **Lord, thank you for creating each of us with such an incredible and unique beauty. Thank you for making everyone in this room special in your eyes. In the remaining time we have together, I ask that you help each of us discover the unique person you created us to be so that we can be true to ourselves and to you. In Jesus' name, amen.**

■ Getting Your Bearings

(10 to 15 minutes)
Supplies: Paper, pencils

Say: **Before you can set a course for the future, you have to know where you are. Let's take some time to discover who we are right now by looking at the roles we play in our lives.**

Have students form groups of four or fewer, and give each group paper and pencils. Then say: **Everyone take a sheet of paper and secretly write on it all the roles you play in life. For example, you're playing the role of a student right now. You also play roles in your family, at work, and with your friends. Try to list at least five roles you play, but don't list more than ten. And don't let any of your group members see your list yet.**

When everyone has finished, say: **Now you're going to tell your fellow group members about the roles you wrote down. But you're not going to tell them in the ordinary way. Instead, you're going to act out a few of the roles you wrote down.**

Have group members take turns acting out two or three of the roles they wrote down, and let the rest of the group guess the roles.

When everyone has finished, ask:

● **What was difficult about this activity?**

● **How is acting out roles like trying to live without a clear sense of who you are?**

● **How can developing a personal life code help you live with moral character as God wants you to?**

● **How can understanding the roles you play in life help you develop a personal life code?**

Say: **The roles you play in life can be like the sails on your sailboat. When all the sails are working together, the boat can catch more wind and travel faster toward your goal. But when the sails are turned in different directions, the boat can flounder in the water and get stuck. That's why understanding the roles you play in life can be so important.**

Have students find a partner and discuss these questions:

● **Are there any roles you play in life that you think aren't good for you? Explain.**

● **Are there any roles you don't have that you think would be good for you to have? Explain.**

Have people change their lists of roles based on their responses to these questions by adding roles they think would benefit them and by eliminating roles that are detrimental.

■ Checking the Sail

(10 to 15 minutes)

Supplies: Bibles, paper, scissors, markers, tape

Say: **Now that we all have a working list of roles we play in life, I want you each to use the supplies I gave you to create a new sail for your boat that lists a lifetime goal for each of the roles on your list. For example, if one of your roles is "son" or "daughter," your lifetime goal for that role could be something like, "I want to be known as someone who always honored my parents."**

To help people create their goals, have them read together Deuteronomy 5:6-21 and Hebrews 12:1-2. Say: **Use these passages as a guide for creating your goals.**

As people complete their sails, have them attach the sails to their boats and explain their goals to their group members. Encourage group members to discuss their goals by sharing what they like about each other's goals and by making suggestions for how the goals could be strengthened.

When groups are finished, say: **Congratulations! You're now well on your way to creating a personal life code. God wants you to have moral character, and setting goals like these can help you do that in a powerful way.**

If some people have trouble coming up with lifetime goals for their roles, suggest that they begin writing their goals with the phrase, "I want to be known as someone who..." This will help people think through what's most important to them concerning each role on their lists.

■ Setting a Course

(5 to 10 minutes)

Supplies: "My Life Code" handouts (p. 75), pencils

Say: **Now you're ready to embark on the final stage of our process— creating an overall "life code" based on all the roles you identified. But creating a life code is no small task, and it's going to take each of you some time and thought to create one for yourself that both challenges you and pleases God. But don't worry. You don't have to do it alone. Your friends here are going to help you.**

Distribute pencils and copies of the "My Life Code" handout. Say: **This handout is designed to be a guide to help you create an overall personal life code based on all the discoveries we've made so far. After looking over the handout, I want you to work with your group to pick a time and place to meet so you can work together to create a personal life code for each person in your group.**

Doing this important task with your group is important for two reasons. First, you can benefit from each other's input and help each other create the best life code possible. And second, once your

Biblical Background

Hebrews 12:1-2 provides a challenging starting point for young adults as they begin to think about developing a personal life code that will guide their choices and priorities. That's because the passage so clearly defines what must be the ultimate priority in life for anyone who claims the title of "Christian"—even if that means letting go of other lesser priorities that are meaningful to us as individuals.

Consider this quote from Christian singer and writer Michael Card in his book *Immanuel:* "Almost everyone who follows Jesus in the New Testament leaves something behind for His sake. Simon and the other disciples who were fishermen left their nets and boats. James and John, the sons of Zebedee, left their father in the process as well as a prosperous family business…Matthew left behind an even more lucrative business, tax gathering…Once Matthew left his wealth to follow Jesus we never hear him mention money or power again!

"You can go on and on. The farther down the path you get, the higher the possessions piled on either side. With each object the travelers left behind, and leave behind, a small piece of themselves, because a possession isn't a little something you own, as much as something that owns a little bit of you. We leave behind a part of our old self, our 'old man.' In return for whatever small thing we discard Jesus gives us a part of Himself in exchange. With Him is great freedom from those things we leave behind, freedom from that greatest self-possessing possession, our 'self.' "

As you consider leading people to create a personal life code that focuses on Jesus, remind them that there will certainly be things in their lives they will have to leave behind.

Leader tip

A few weeks after this study, check in with people to see whether they've completed their life codes. Then, over the next several months, ask some people to tell the group how creating a life code has impacted their lives.

life codes are complete, you can help each other stick to them in the coming year.

Have people follow the instructions in part 1 of the handout. When they're finished, have them pray together for each individual in their group, asking God to help him or her be faithful to building moral character by setting a godly course for his or her life.

My Life Code
h a n d o u t

Part 1

As a group, decide on a time and place to meet to create your own personal life code. After your initial meeting, you may want to get together again a week or so later to make any additional changes you think would strengthen your life code.

When we'll meet:

Where we'll meet:

Remember to bring this handout, your sailboat, your Bible, and a pencil with you!

Part 2

"Therefore, since we are surrounded by such a great cloud of witnesses, let us throw off everything that hinders and the sin that so easily entangles, and let us run with perseverance the race marked out for us. Let us fix our eyes on Jesus, the author and perfecter of our faith, who for the joy set before him endured the cross, scorning its shame, and sat down at the right hand of the throne of God" (Hebrews 12:1-2).

Follow the instructions below, and work with your group to create your own personal life code.
1. Read through the Scripture passage above, and tell the group at least three things about the passage that can help you create a life code that would please God.
2. Read through the goals you created at the group meeting; then use them to guide you as you write an answer to this question:
● What do you want people to remember about you after you die?
3. Use the information from step 2, along with your goals from the group meeting, to create a personal life code on the back of this sheet. Try to keep your code brief—no more than ten or twelve lines long.

Takin' Care of Busyness

Finding Peace in a Too-Busy World

 BIBLICAL POINT: God helps you deal with suffering.
BIBLE BASIS: Luke 10:38-42; Luke 22:39-46; Philippians 4:12-13
TOPIC: Busyness

Beep! Beep! Beep…
From the time their alarm clocks get them scrambling out of bed in the morning until their heads drop to their pillows at night, young adults are on the go. Work or school, responsibilities with families and homes, church activities, sports or other hobbies…people today seem to run at the speed of light.

But for all this flurry of activity, studies show that people today feel less connected, more lost, and more depressed than ever before.

No matter how busy life gets, people can't afford to ignore their stress or their suffering. They need reassurance that someone is always there, ready to listen and comfort. This study encourages people to take time from their busy lives to lean on the One who can best help them deal with their suffering.

 Before the study, photocopy the "Chaos Cards" handout (p. 84)—one for every four students—and cut out enough cards so each person can have one set of directions. Cut adding machine tape into four-inch lengths. Make enough strips for each person in the study to have one, plus a few extras. If you don't have adding machine tape, cut two-by-four-inch strips from regular sheets of paper.

Use the "Jesus' Last Day" box (p. 81) to create on newsprint a time line of the last twenty-four hours before Jesus' crucifixion. Keep this time line hidden until the activity calls for it.

Also tape several large sheets of newsprint to the walls of the room, and scatter assorted colors of markers below each sheet.

You'll also need
● Bibles,

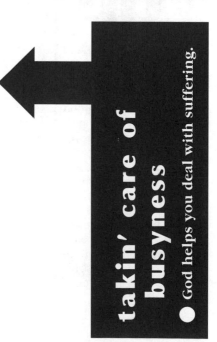

takin' care of busyness

● God helps you deal with suffering.

- one "Daily Planner Page" handout (p. 84) for each person,
- pencils,
- a watch, and
- a large cup.

Leader tip ▼

It's OK if people finish their tasks early or if they can't complete all of them. Whatever their status at the end of two minutes, students will have sensed the chaotic mood, and the varied experiences will add to the discussion.

■ Chaos Encounter

(15 to 20 minutes)

Supplies: Bibles, "Daily Planner Page" handouts (p. 84), pencils, "Chaos Cards" handouts (p. 84), watch, strips of adding machine tape

When everyone has arrived, give each student a "Daily Planner Page" handout and a pencil. Say: **Based on conversations we've had, I know we lead very busy lives. Using your planner page, write down what you do in a typical day from the time you wake up until the time you go to sleep.** After everyone has finished, have people set aside their handouts for use later in the study.

Then say: **Now we're going to play a game. I'll give each of you a card containing a set of instructions, and you'll have two minutes to fully complete all the tasks on your card.** Hand each person a set of instructions from the "Chaos Cards" handout; then say: **I'll be keeping the official time on my watch. Ready? Go!**

As people perform their tasks, create a chaotic mood by frequently calling out the time remaining. Also walk into the center of the room holding the strips of paper you prepared before the study. Make paper wads from the strips, and toss them randomly at peoples' feet. Leave the wads where they fall, and allow students to react to the wads however they wish.

After two minutes, call time. Then have students form trios to discuss these questions:

● **What was your reaction to this game?**

● **How was trying to finish all your tasks like living a busy life? How was it different?**

● **How were the wads of paper I threw at you like problems you face daily? How were they different?**

● **What was your response when I threw the paper wads? Why?**

● **How was that response like your response to personal problems that arise in your busy life? How was it different?**

After trios have finished discussing the questions, invite students to share their insights with everyone. Then say: **Sometimes we fill our lives with so many activities and responsibilities that we end up pushing aside some of our most important issues. And just like those paper wads lying on the floor, our suffering doesn't disappear if we ignore it or are too busy to deal with it. Let's see what Jesus says about busyness.**

Have students return to their trios, and have one volunteer in each trio read aloud Luke 10:38-42. Then have trios discuss these questions:

Leader tip ▼

When you throw the paper wads, students' reactions will vary. Whether the entire group stops to acknowledge you, people don't notice the wads, or people respond in a variety of ways, don't discourage them. If you allow them to respond naturally, they'll have meaningful insights for the subsequent discussion.

● **Why do you think Mary and Martha reacted differently to Jesus' presence?**

● **What did Jesus say about that difference?**

● **Who are you more like: Mary or Martha? Why?**

● **Based on this Scripture, how do you think Mary would react to suffering in her life? What about Martha? Explain.**

● **From what you experienced in our game and from what Jesus said about Mary and Martha, what do you think would be a good response to suffering in your life? Explain.**

Say: **Putting aside busyness to face something painful can be really difficult. It forces us to feel the pain we'd much rather avoid. Fortunately, we don't have to face our suffering alone. God helps us deal with suffering; all we need to do is take the time to allow him to work in our lives.**

Biblical Background

The story of Mary and Martha from Luke 10:38-42 demonstrates the importance of spending time with God. Mary's stirring act of devotion here—and Jesus' response to it—is strengthened further by the fact that Mary behaved in a way uncharacteristic for women of the day. With the arrival of important guests such as Jesus and his disciples, a woman would typically respond as Martha did, adopting the hostess role. Mary, however, took a place at Jesus' feet. This posture indicated discipleship—a male role—and would have "shocked most Jewish men." Jesus, however, welcomed Mary's attention. Although Martha's activity represented her devotion to Jesus, Mary's indicated even higher values. Jesus defended and complimented Mary's choice, encouraging her and Martha to seek God (Craig S. Keener, *The IVP Bible Background Commentary: New Testament*).

■ T-Minus 24 Hours

(15 to 20 minutes)

Supplies: Bibles, markers, tape

Gather everyone around you, and say: **Let's explore this idea a little further. Suppose you know you have only twenty-four hours left to live and that at the end of those twenty-four hours you'll be cruelly and painfully murdered. Think about all the things you'd want to accomplish in those last twenty-four hours—people you'd want to say goodbye to, places you'd want to go, things you'd want to do. Scatter around the room to the sheets of newsprint hanging on the walls, and find a space to write. Then create a time line of everything you'd want to achieve in your last twenty-four hours, beginning at 3 p.m. one day and ending at 3 p.m. the next. You have five minutes to complete your time line.**

While students write, pick up the paper wads you dropped on the floor in the "Chaos Encounter" activity, and set them aside to use later.

After five minutes, call time, and gather everyone together. Bring out the time line of Jesus' last twenty-four hours (that you created before the study), and tape it to a wall in front of the group.

Say: **This time line shows what Jesus did during his last twenty-four hours on earth. Jesus knew he had only twenty-four hours left; he knew he would be cruelly, painfully, unfairly murdered; and he knew who his murderers would be. With that background, let's see how Jesus chose to spend those last, precious twenty-four hours.** Read the time line aloud, giving special emphasis to Jesus' time of prayer in the Garden of Gethsemane. Then have students form groups of four to discuss these questions:

● **Compared to your predicted last day on earth, how busy was Jesus' last day?**

● **Why do you think Jesus chose to go to the Garden of Gethsemane to pray?**

● **Read Luke 22:39-46. According to this passage, how do you think Jesus felt about what was going to happen to him?**

● **How did he deal with those feelings?**

Say: **Jesus tried to accomplish a lot in the twenty-four hours before his crucifixion. But in the middle of that painful, difficult day, he set aside time to take his cup of suffering to God. He knew that to endure his crucifixion, he'd have to rely on his Father because God helps us deal with suffering.**

Have foursomes discuss these questions:

● **Why do you think Jesus confronted rather than avoided his suffering?**

● **Look at your time line. In your last twenty-four hours, would you have confronted your suffering? Why or why not?**

● **What might be the dangers of confronting suffering? What might be the benefits?**

● **What can you learn from Jesus' example?**

Say: **God will help us deal with the suffering we face in our lives if we allow him to. For that reason, no matter how busy we are, we must slow down long enough to take our cup of suffering to God.**

■ Cup of Suffering

(10 to 15 minutes)

Supplies: Pencils, paper wads from the "Chaos Encounters" activity, a large cup

Hand each person a pencil and a paper wad. Ask students to scatter throughout the room so that each person can be alone. After people have settled into their own spaces, say: **We all face personal suffering, and when we stop to think, we often discover problems we've been avoiding. As difficult as this is, let's give it a try right now. Flatten out your paper wad, and write on it something you worry about or a problem you face. Then**

Jesus' Last Day

No person knew more about dealing with suffering under pressure than Jesus. In his final hours, Jesus had to prepare his disciples for his death, and he had to warn them of the suffering they'd face after he was gone. In the midst of this frenzy and with the knowledge of a looming, horrible death, Jesus knew he had to spend time with his Father, and he did so at Gethsemane.

This time line will help students realize how they can always take time to bring their suffering—regardless of the gravity of their problems—to God.

Thursday, 3 p.m.–10 p.m.

Jesus prepares for the Passover meal (Luke 22:7-13).

Jesus shares the Last Supper with his disciples (Luke 22:14-22).

Jesus washes his disciples' feet (John 13:1-17).

Thursday, 10 p.m.–12 a.m.

Jesus prays in the Garden of Gethsemane (Luke 22:39-46).

Judas betrays Jesus (Luke 22:47-48).

Jesus heals the priest's servant (Luke 22:49-51).

Jesus is arrested (Luke 22:52-54a).

Friday, 12:30 a.m.–2:30 a.m.

Three times Peter denies knowing Jesus (Luke 22:55-62).

Jesus faces mocking by the soldiers who guard him at a high priest's house (Luke 22:63-65).

Friday, sunrise

Jesus is put on trial by elders (Luke 22:66-71).

Friday, morning

Jesus goes before Pilate (Luke 23:1-5).

Jesus goes before Herod (Luke 23:6-11a).

Jesus goes before Pilate a second time, is rejected by the crowd, and is sentenced to death (Luke 23:11b-25).

Friday, 12 p.m.–3 p.m.

Jesus walks to The Skull, teaching along the way (Luke 23:26-31).

Jesus is crucified (Luke 23:33).

Jesus asks God to forgive his enemies (Luke 23:34).

Jesus dies on the cross (Luke 23:44-46).

(Source: Craig S. Keener, *The IVP Bible Background Commentary: New Testament*)

Leader tip ▼

To ensure that you'll have enough room in the cup for every paper, make sure people fold their papers instead of crumpling them into wads again. If you have a large study and need a larger container, substitute a paper bag or a large pitcher.

fold up your paper. Give people a couple of minutes to think and write, and fill out a paper wad yourself. Then have everyone form a circle together and then sit down. Hold up the large cup, and say: **Though facing our suffering is difficult, we don't have to endure it alone. God helps us deal with suffering when we allow him to.**

We're going to pass this cup around the circle. When the cup comes to you, you have the choice of putting your paper in the cup as a symbol of handing your problem to God. If you choose to put your paper in the cup, say the following as you do so: "Lord, please take this cup of suffering." Start with yourself; then pass the cup to a person sitting next to you.

When the cup returns to you, have people form pairs to discuss these questions:

● **How did you feel when you had the choice of handing your problem to God?**

● **How will this experience affect what you do with personal suffering on a daily basis?**

Then have each person pray for his or her partner, asking for God's help in making time to deal with suffering. After a minute, finish the prayer for the whole group by praying aloud: **Dear God, thank you for helping us deal with our suffering. Help us to remember to make time in our busy lives to bring our cup of suffering to you. Amen.**

■ Prayer Planning

(5 to 10 minutes)

Supplies: A Bible, "Daily Planner Page" handouts from the "Chaos Encounters" activity, pencils

Have people retrieve their planner pages from the first activity, and hand out pencils. Say: **Paul, a great disciple, was imprisoned many times for teaching others about Jesus. I'm going to read an excerpt of a letter he wrote from prison to a congregation of Christians.** Read aloud Philippians 4:12-13. Say: **Paul suffered for his faith and for telling others about Jesus. But through his faith in Jesus, he found the strength he needed to continue with high spirits. God helped Paul deal with his suffering, and God will help you deal with suffering, too. All you have to do is make the time to bring your problems to him.**

Look at your daily planner page. If you didn't include some time to spend with God in your typical day, you may choose to pencil time in now. Pause for people to do this if they want. **Now, on the top of your sheet in the "Don't Forget:" space, write Philippians 4:13: "I can do everything through him who gives me strength."** Encourage students to take their daily planner pages home and place them where their pages can remind them to spend time with God every day.

Paul's Secret of Happiness

The Apostle Paul faced more than his fair share of suffering. He was imprisoned many times for teaching others about Christ. He was beaten. He was denounced by fellow Jews, misunderstood by fellow Christians, and ostracized by Gentiles. He had more than enough reason to give in to fear and hatred. But Paul didn't wither or fade or fall into hatred. In fact, he lived with a deeply felt joy, and he communicated that joy in his letter to the Philippians. Despite the fact that Paul wrote this New Testament book while imprisoned in Rome, "The entire letter breathes Paul's radiant joy and serene happiness in Christ, even while in prison and in danger of death" (*The New Oxford Annotated Bible With the Apocrypha*).

How did Paul keep such an admirable attitude under these dire circumstances? In Philippians 4:13, Paul revealed his secret: "I can do everything through him who gives me strength."

What a powerful example for all of us! Paul found joy despite burdensome circumstances because he took his suffering to God, and God gave him the strength he needed to endure it.

"I know what it is to be in need, and I know what it is to have plenty. I have learned the secret of being content in any and every situation, whether well fed or hungry, whether living in plenty or in want. I can do everything through him who gives me strength."
—Philippians 4:12-13

Daily Planner Page

handout

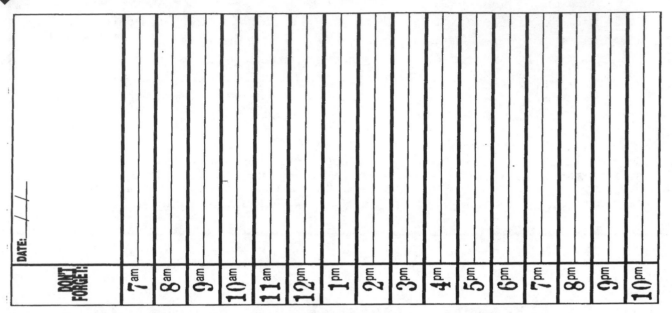

DATE: __/__/__

DON'T FORGET:

7am | 8am | 9am | 10am | 11am | 12pm | 1pm | 2pm | 3pm | 4pm | 5pm | 6pm | 7pm | 8pm | 9pm | 10pm

Chaos Cards

handout

Card 1

1. Find two people wearing red, and pay each a compliment.
2. Tell someone you don't know very well what your favorite holiday is and why.
3. Walk around the room backward twice while humming the national anthem.
4. Read Luke 10:38-42.

Card 3

1. Find two people wearing white, and pay each a compliment.
2. Tell someone with glasses what your favorite TV show is and why.
3. Pantomime a scene from *The Wizard of Oz*.
4. Read Luke 10:38-42.

Card 2

1. Find two people wearing blue, and pay each a compliment.
2. Sing your favorite Christmas carol to a member of the opposite sex.
3. "Skate" a figure eight while balancing a Bible on your head.
4. Read Luke 10:38-42.

Card 4

1. Find two people wearing black, and pay each a compliment.
2. Sing "Happy Birthday" in an Elmer Fudd voice to someone with brown hair.
3. Do jumping jacks from one end of the room to the other end.
4. Read Luke 10:38-42.

The End of the World

BIBLICAL POINT: You can be ready for Christ's return.

BIBLE BASIS: Revelation 2–3

TOPIC: Priorities

We all live in a fast-paced world. We pay bills that are due tomorrow (or yesterday), add new chores daily to our to-do lists, and barely find time to squeeze in that all-important "Must See TV" episode. But rarely do we find or make time to set real priorities—much less act on them.

This study brings the issue of priorities into focus with the reminder that any day could be our last; any day could be the day Christ returns. Will we be ready?

In this study, students will discover the priorities that the risen Christ gave to seven churches preparing for his return. By examining how biblical priorities can be applied to their lives, people can identify ways to change their own priorities and gain the assurance that they can be ready for Christ's return.

Before the study, gather together the following supplies:

- Bibles,
- pens,
- seven "Profile: Believers at _____" handouts (p. 91),
- paper,
- pencils,
- markers, and
- white stones.

■ Pressures and Priorities

(up to 5 minutes)

Supplies: None needed

Have people form groups of four, and have each person complete these sentences:

- **One thing I absolutely have to get done this week is...**
- **One thing I'd love to find the time to do this week is...**
- **Anybody who watches how I spend my time this week would say my top priority is...**

the end of the world

● You can be ready for Christ's return.

Once groups are finished, ask the entire group:

● **What would you say are the top priorities of people you interact with during the day?**

● **Are the priorities of Christians different from non-Christians? Explain.**

● **If you knew you would die the day after tomorrow, what would you do?**

Say: **The book of Revelation contains seven letters that instruct Christians how to live expectantly, as though Jesus could return tomorrow—or even within the next hour. Today we'll investigate those letters to determine priorities that will help us be ready for Christ's return.**

■ Fact-Finding Teams

(15 to 20 minutes)

Supplies: Bibles, pens, "Profile: Believers at _____" handouts (p. 91)

Have people form seven teams, and assign one of the seven churches in Revelation 2–3 to each team:

● Ephesus (EF-eh-sus) from Revelation 2:1-7
● Smyrna (SMUR-na) from Revelation 2:8-11)
● Pergamum (PER-guh-mum) from Revelation 2:12-17)
● Thyatira (THY-ah-TY-rah) from Revelation 2:18-29)
● Sardis (SAR-dis) from Revelation 3:1-6)
● Philadelphia (Fill-uh-DEL-fee-uh) from Revelation 3:7-13)
● Laodicea (Lay-ah-deh-SEE-uh) from Revelation 3:14-22)

Distribute Bibles, pens, and one copy of the "Profile: Believers at _____" handout to each team. Have each team complete the handout for its assigned church. As teams work, circulate and answer any questions students have about their assignments. Share with them the appropriate information from the "Profile Possibilities" box (p. 87) and the "Who Were These Bad Guys?" box (p. 88).

■ Investigative Reports

(5 to 10 minutes)

Supplies: None needed

As teams finish their profiles, have each prepare a "TV presentation" that will report all the information in their profiles. Let teams be as creative as they like in choosing the TV format. For example, they could create their own versions of TV dramas, news shows, or talk shows. Teams could even present their information while acting out their favorite sitcoms or soap operas. As people work, be sure to limit preparation time so they have time for the rest of the study.

After about ten minutes of preparation time, have each team present its investigative report. After the final report, say: **The churches in these letters probably took the priorities seriously so they'd be ready for Christ's**

Leader tip

If your group is too small to form seven teams, assign each team more than one church to profile. Since seven churches don't divide evenly, you can even out the workload by giving fewer churches to the team that studies the last letter (Laodicea). That letter involves symbolism that may take a little more time to understand.

Leader tip

If students need help deciding how to present their report, bring the whole group together to list their seven favorite TV shows. Then assign each team one of the shows to role play as the vehicle for sharing the information they gathered. (Picture, for example, paramedics rushing the church of Laodicea through the halls of "ER" while the doctor exclaims, "The patient is neither hot nor cold!")

Profile Possibilities

In the "Fact-Finding Teams" activity, some teams might have trouble creating their church profiles. If that happens, use this information from Revelation to help students understand the message behind their assigned letter.

Ephesus
- Good stuff: They work hard and never give up (2:2); they don't put up with false teachings (2:2); they hate what the Nicolaitans* do (2:6).
- Bad stuff: They left the love they had (2:4).
- Charge: To change their hearts and love as they once did (2:5).
- Possible priority: Renew their passion for God.

Smyrna
- Good stuff: Although they're materially poor, they're spiritually rich (2:9).
- Bad stuff: None.
- Charge: To not be afraid of what you have to suffer and to be faithful until death (2:10).
- Possible priority: Express their faith even when it's unpopular.

Pergamum
- Good stuff: They have stayed true to Christ; they don't refuse to tell about faith (2:13).
- Bad stuff: Some follow Balaam and the Nicolaitans* (2:14-15).
- Charge: To change their hearts and leave behind those sins (2:16).
- Possible priority: Examine themselves for sin and get rid of it.

Thyatira
- Good stuff: They promote love, faith, service, patience (2:19).
- Bad stuff: They allow Jezebel* to spread false teachings; commit sexual sins, and eat food sacrificed to idols (2:20).
- Charge: To turn away from wrongs (2:22) and to stay loyal (2:25).
- Possible priority: Look for ways to demonstrate their loyalty to Christ through service, sexual morality, and love.

Sardis
- Good stuff: A few have remained morally unstained (3:4).
- Bad stuff: They're spiritually dead; they're doing less than God wants (3:1-2).
- Charge: To make themselves stronger; to not forget; to obey (3:2-3).
- Possible priority: Study what God says and then do it.

Philadelphia
- Good stuff: They obey and aren't afraid to speak Christ's name (3:8).
- Bad stuff: None.
- Charge: To continue strong in faith (3:11).
- Possible priority: Tell others about Christ.

Laodicea
- Good stuff: None.
- Bad stuff: They're lukewarm—indifferent about Christ (3:16).
- Charge: To buy gold (seek spiritual wealth, not material wealth), white clothes (a symbol for moral purity), medicine for their eyes (spiritual discernment and understanding); to open the door to Christ (3:18, 20).
- Possible priority: Receive Christ if they haven't; become "fired up" about Christ, not lukewarm.

(*See the "Who Were These Bad Guys?" box on page 88.)

Who Were These Bad Guys?

In the Revelation passages, students will read about several "bad guys" God didn't approve of. If people aren't familiar with these people or groups, use this information to help fill the gaps.

● **The Nicolaitans** (Revelation 2:6, 15) abused Christian liberty to engage in sexual immorality and other vices.

● **Balak** (Revelation 2:14) was a king of Moab who commanded **Balaam** to curse Israel (Numbers 22–24). Later, Balaam urged the Moabites to lure Israel into immorality and idolatry (Numbers 25:1-2; 31:16).

● **Jezebel** (Revelation 2:20) was a queen who led Israel to worship Baal (1 Kings 16:31). Her name represents false prophets who lead believers astray.

Biblical Background

According to one of the "Sidelight" commentaries in The Youth Bible, "The island of Patmos, where John wrote Revelation (Revelation 1:9), was the Alcatraz of the Roman Empire. Religious and political prisoners were banished to this island prison, which is only about ten miles long."

A Christian preacher like John would have been low in the prison hierarchy and would most likely have been subjected to hard labor in the quarries. (Source: Morris, Leon. *Revelation.* Tyndale New Testament Commentaries Series. Eerdmans, 1987.)

return. We're not in such a different situation—we don't know when Christ is coming back. It could be years from now, or it could be any day. Let's see how the priorities in these letters apply to us.

■ Letters to Individuals

(15 to 20 minutes)

Supplies: Paper, pencils

After the investigative reports, post the church profiles in different places around the room. Then have people go to the churches whose situations and priorities they most identify with.

Within the new groups formed at each church, form pairs and give each person paper and a pencil.

Have each person write a short letter to his or her partner, using the format of the letters to the churches ("I know these good things about you…" followed by "Make this a priority…"). For example, "I know these good things about you…that you're honest and kind, and you always listen when people need to talk. Make this a priority…keep focusing on God, and don't forget to take time for yourself."

When people finish, have them give their scrolls to each other to read privately.

■ A New Name

(5 to 10 minutes)

Supplies: Bibles, markers, white stones

When everyone is finished, call the group together, and say: **You can be ready for Christ's return. And being ready will affect your day-to-day priorities. Think about what priority you especially need to focus on this week and how you'll focus on it.**

After a minute or two for reflection, read aloud Revelation 2:17. Then say: **Think of a "new name" you could call yourself if you achieved your goal of acting on your priority—for example, "she who never gives up" (Revelation 2:2) or "brave teller" (Revelation 2:13).**

Give everyone a white stone and a marker, and let people write their new names or draw reminders of their priorities on the stones. Sit in a circle, and have each person find out the priority and new name of the person on the right. Then go around the circle, letting each person pray for the person on the right, asking that the person live up to the new name he or she has chosen. After the prayer, have each student tell the person on the right one way they see God's favor working in his or her life.

Biblical Background

In ancient times, a defendant on trial was given a black stone if he or she was found guilty and a white stone if he or she was found innocent. Stones were also sometimes used as tickets to royal feasts. Either way, the white stone represents God's favor.

(Source: *The Quest Study Bible*)

Biblical Background

Although this study focuses on the seven letters recorded in Revelation 2 and 3, there are many Scripture passages that admonish Christians to be ready for Christ's return. Here's just a sampling:

Matthew 24:42-44	"Therefore keep watch, because you do not know on what day your Lord will come. But understand this: If the owner of the house had known at what time of night the thief was coming, he would have kept watch and would not have let his house be broken into. So you also must be ready, because the Son of Man will come at an hour when you do not expect him."
Mark 13:26, 32-33	"At that time men will see the Son of Man coming in clouds with great power and glory…No one knows about that day or hour, not even the angels in heaven, nor the Son, but only the Father. Be on guard! Be alert! You do not know when that time will come."
Romans 13:11-14	"And do this, understanding the present time. The hour has come for you to wake up from your slumber, because our salvation is nearer now than when we first believed. The night is nearly over; the day is almost here. So let us put aside the deeds of darkness and put on the armour of light. Let us behave decently, as in the daytime, not in orgies and drunkenness, not in sexual immorality and debauchery, not in dissension and jealousy. Rather, clothe yourselves with the Lord Jesus Christ, and do not think about how to gratify the desires of the sinful nature."
1 Thessalonians 5:1-2,6	"Now, brothers, about times and dates we do not need to write to you, for you know very well that the day of the Lord will come like a thief in the night…So then, let us not be like others, who are asleep, but let us be alert and self-controlled."
2 Peter 3:11-12a	"Since everything will be destroyed in this way, what kind of people ought you to be? You ought to live holy and godly lives as you look forward to the day of God and speed its coming."

Profile:
Believers at _____

handout

Your team has an assignment in investigative journalism: to piece together a profile of a church based on an ancient letter written to that church.

Read the letter that was written to your assigned church, then gather the following information. If you have questions about obscure language or references, ask your leader for additional insight.

● The good stuff they were doing:

● The bad stuff they were doing:

● Christ's charge to them:

Investigative reporting isn't complete without drawing some conclusions from the data gathered. Determine one or two priorities you think Christ had for this church by examining the good stuff, the bad stuff, and the charge.

● Priority 1:

● Priority 2 (optional):

The Meaning of Life

Discovering Your Ultimate Purpose

BIBLICAL POINT: God's Spirit reveals your true purpose in life.
BIBLE BASIS: Proverbs 3:5-6; 4:18-19; 1 Corinthians 2:11-12; Colossians 3:12-17
TOPIC: Purpose

introduction

For the first time in their lives, most of your group members are on their own. For the first time, the decisions are theirs, the future is theirs, the responsibility is theirs.

While this new freedom can be exciting, most young adults feel a little lost. They're not really sure what they're supposed to do with their lives or what their purpose is—and they're not sure how to find the answers. The result may be experimentation or stagnation.

What a sense of peace they'll find when they learn that God has a plan for them and is here to support them.

This study takes students on a journey through their past, present, and future. They'll create three-dimensional time lines to try to discover the sense of purpose and security that comes from following the Holy Spirit and allowing him to reveal God's vision for their lives.

 Before this study, gather the following supplies:
● Bibles,
● colored paper,
● markers,
● tape,
● newsprint,
● yarn,
● pens,
● scissors, and
● one "Looking Back to Find Your Purpose" handout (p. 97) for each person.

the meaning of life
● God's Spirit reveals your true purpose in life.

■ Community Builder

(up to 5 minutes)

Supplies: Colored paper, markers, tape

As students arrive, give them each a sheet of colored paper and a marker. On their papers, ask students to write their names, their birth dates, and one reason they think God created them. When they finish, have them find partners. Then have partners share the information on their papers and tell each other another positive reason they think God created their partners.

Distribute tape, and ask people to post their papers at random locations on the walls, ceiling, or floor. Then say: **Most of us wonder at times, "What's my purpose in life?" Well today we're going to explore our lives in a creative way to discover more about our purpose in life. Our family members, teachers, or employers may think they can tell us what our purpose is, but we need to consult someone who knows everything about us: God's Spirit reveals our true purpose in life. And by following God, we can discover not only why he created us but also what he wants us to become.**

Understanding Your Students

When you talk with young adults about their "ultimate purpose" in life, consider their perspective on the future. Neil Howe, an author and expert on generational trends, said in an interview, "I think what you need to have to work successfully with [this age group] is the ability to understand that the objectives of today's [young people] are very real and important to them. They're [facing] questions of survival—getting by in a world that really doesn't want them, in a world in which so many of the social rituals from courtship and marriage to economic opportunities…don't work for them anymore. So older people have to understand that these are issues of tremendous significance."

■ Creative Project

(20 to 25 minutes)

Supplies: Colored paper, newsprint, yarn, tape, pens, scissors

Say: **To begin our exploration, let's first look into the past.**

Distribute three sheets of colored paper to each person. Then say: **Think about your past, and pick out three periods in your life when you've experienced dramatic change—for example, when your parents divorced, when you moved from one place to another, or when a serious relationship began or ended. You decide.**

Once everyone has decided, say: **Now on each sheet of paper, write a paragraph, draw a picture, or create a symbol that represents one of those major life changes. Then below your creation, describe what you think your purpose in life was during that time.**

While students are working, place a sheet of newsprint that the whole group can gather around on the floor. If the study is especially large or if the room is small, lay out several sheets of newsprint for smaller groups to gather around. In the center of the newsprint, write "Here and Now."

After students finish their creations, distribute tape again, and have people post their sheets at random locations on the walls, ceiling, or floor.

Then say: **Now let's take what we've done and create a time line or "lifeline" of our lives.**

Set out scissors, tape, and several skeins of different colors of yarn, and tell people to use the yarn to connect, in chronological order, the sheets of paper that describe their lives. Once everyone has connected all four sheets with yarn, have people find partners and take each other on four-minute tours of their lives. Make sure people explain each sheet and describe how they viewed their purpose in life during each situation.

While pairs are taking tours, find an open place on one of the meeting room walls, and tape a large sheet of newsprint on it. Along the top of the newsprint, write "My Ultimate Purpose."

Encourage students to cut a separate strand of yarn to connect each section of their lifelines. That way, if one strand accidentally comes down, it won't destroy the entire lifeline.

■ Here and Now

(up to 5 minutes)

Supplies: Bibles, markers, yarn, tape, "Looking Back to Find Your Purpose" handouts (p. 97)

When pairs finish their tours, have everyone go to the newsprint you've titled "Here and Now," write his or her name, and draw a circle around the name. Then have students tape strings of yarn from their last sheets of paper to the circles they've created. In their circles, have people write what they think might be their purpose in life this year.

When they finish, distribute Bibles and copies of the "Looking Back to Find Your Purpose" handout. Have people find new partners. After sharing what they wrote in the circles on the "Here and Now" newsprint, have pairs go through the handout together.

■ Ultimate Meaning

(15 to 20 minutes)

Supplies: Bibles, yarn, tape, newsprint, markers

When pairs finish their handouts, have everyone trace their left hands on the newsprint titled "My Ultimate Purpose." Have each person use another length of yarn to connect their circled names on the "Here and Now" newsprint to their left hand prints. Then have pairs read together Colossians 3:12-17 and Romans 12:1-2. Then say: **Based on these passages, write in your new circle what you believe is God's ultimate purpose for all of our lives.**

When people finish, ask several volunteers to explain what they've written. Then have the group look at the tangled web of yarn it has created throughout the room. Say: **From our point of view, life can look a**

Leader tip ▼

If the responses students write on the newsprint are drastically different from the idea that God's ultimate purpose is for us to become like Jesus, take a moment to ask them why they've chosen those answers. Invite them to support their responses based on Scripture. Then pray as a group, asking God for his wisdom as you search together to find God's ultimate purpose for your lives.

lot like this room. Choices can take us in random directions, and it can often seem like no one guides our lives. But God doesn't see things the way we do. He isn't confused by life's many uncertain twists and turns. When we follow his Spirit, the Spirit will show us God's true purpose for our lives.

Have students look at what they've written on the "My Ultimate Purpose" newsprint while you read aloud Colossians 3:12-17. Then say: **God's ultimate purpose for all of us is that we become like his Son, Jesus. What we do, where we live, how we make a living—all of that is secondary to God's ultimate purpose: that each of us live like his Son.**

■ Personal Reflection

(up to 5 minutes)
Supplies: None needed

Have people start at the final sheet of newsprint and retrace their lifelines backward through time. Each time they come within three feet of another person's lifeline, have them tell that person one reason they're glad he or she has "crossed paths" with them in life or one way that person has shown them how to live like Jesus. Make sure every student is affirmed.

Say: **God's Spirit reveals our true purpose in life, and often that revelation comes through the people around us who show what it means to live like Jesus.**

■ Commitment

(up to 5 minutes)
Supplies: None needed

After everyone has retraced his or her lifeline, have people reflect silently about this question:

● **How would my daily life change if I were more committed to following God's ultimate purpose for my life?**

Then say: **Every day this week, pray for God to change your heart so you can be more committed to his ultimate purpose for your life. Then, when the week is over, choose one way you'll show your new commitment during the next year.**

Close the study by having students form pairs and then pray for each other to commit to pursue God's ultimate purpose for their lives. After the prayer, have partners commit to praying for each other during the coming week.

Looking Back to Find Your Purpose

handout

After you find a partner, go through this handout together to discover how God's Spirit reveals your true purpose in life.

1. Look at the lifeline you've created; then discuss these questions:

● What's your reaction to what you see?

● How are the random directions of your lifeline similar to your search for purpose in life?

● Where have you looked in the past to find purpose in life?

● Where have you looked to try to discover what the future holds for you?

● Do you know your ultimate purpose in life? Why or why not?

● Do you know what your future holds? Why or why not?

● Do you believe God's Spirit reveals your true purpose in life? Why or why not?

● If you absolutely believed that God's Spirit could give you purpose and direction for the future, how would you live differently?

2. Read together Proverbs 3:5-6. In what practical ways can God's Spirit guide your life?

3. Take your partner on a tour of your lifeline. At each stop, tell your partner at least two ways that God's Spirit may have (or could have) led you to make the choices you did. (For example, the Holy Spirit might use circumstances, advice from friends or relatives, or Scripture to guide your choices.) For additional help, read John 16:13 and 1 Corinthians 2:11-12. Then tell your partner how following God's Spirit in the past could've helped (or did help) you discover God's purpose for your future.

4. After your tours, read together Proverbs 4:18-19; then discuss these questions:

● Looking back on your past, how has your purpose in life changed over the years?

● How has God's Spirit used your past experiences to begin to reveal your true purpose in life?

● How has that revelation grown "brighter" over time as this passage describes?

● How does following God's Spirit lessen your fear of the future?

● What do you think is God's ultimate purpose for your life? Explain.

5. Pray with your partner and ask God to reveal his ultimate purpose for your lives during this study.

To Be God... or Godly?

The Quest for True Spirituality

BIBLICAL POINT: Spiritual growth means becoming more like Jesus.

BIBLE BASIS: Psalm 1; John 1:1-5; and Galatians 5:16-26

TOPIC: New Age Movement

Did you know...67 percent of American adults claim to have psychic experiences?... 42 percent of American adults believe they've been in contact with someone who has died?...31 percent believe that some people have magical powers?...thirty million Americans (about one in four) believe in reincarnation?

These statistics are from the book *Understanding the New Age* by Russell Chandler. According to Chandler, a former religion writer for the Los Angeles Times, the New Age movement is probably the most widespread, powerful phenomenon affecting our culture today.

Need more than stats to convince you? Just ask your group members what they think about the beliefs described above.

Their responses may surprise you.

This study contrasts the New Age approach to spirituality with the true spiritual growth described in the Bible. Through this study, your group members will learn to recognize the false spirituality offered by the New Age movement and will discover that becoming more intimate with Jesus Christ is the key to real spiritual growth.

Before the study, form a circle of chairs, and place another chair in the middle of the circle. Make a photocopy of the "True or False Spirituality" box (p. 101), and cut apart the four quotes.

You'll also need

- Bibles,
- tea-light candles,
- matchbooks,
- a large candle,
- paper,
- masking tape,
- yarn,
- assorted nonpermanent markers,
- one "Jesus and Me" handout (p. 105) for each person,
- pencils, and
- newsprint.

to be God...or Godly?

● Spiritual growth means becoming more like Jesus.

Leader tip

Tea-light candles are the small, metal-cupped candles used most often with pot-pourri pots. They give off less light than other candles, but are also less expensive and require no special stand to keep wax from dripping on floors or furniture. If you'd rather use a brighter type of candle, small votive candles also work well and can be placed in small glasses to keep the wax from dripping onto hands or clothes.

■ Creative Comparison

(5 to 10 minutes)

Supplies: Bible, tea-light candles, matchbooks, a large candle, "True or False Spirituality" quotes (p. 101)

Once everyone arrives, have people sit in the circle of chairs. Ask for four volunteers, and give each a tea-light candle, a matchbook, and a quote from the "True or False Spirituality" box. Keep the large candle next to you.

Turn off the lights, and then have the four volunteers light their candles one at a time and read aloud the quotes you provided. When they finish, light the large candle, and slowly read aloud John 1:1-5. When you finish, ask the volunteers to blow out their candles so yours is the only one burning.

Place the candle on the chair in the center of the circle, and have everyone turn to a partner. Then ask:

● **How did each of the quotes—including the one I read—define God or godliness?**

● **How are those definitions similar? different?**

Then read aloud Psalm 1. Ask:

● **What does this passage say about spirituality?**

● **How does this passage compare with the first four quotes we heard?**

Then say: **There are many ideas about what makes you spiritual and what it means to grow spiritually. But the Bible defines spirituality and spiritual growth. Today we're going to explore what it truly means to grow spiritually.**

John 1:5 says, "The light shines in the darkness, but the darkness has not understood it." The candle on the chair represents the light of Jesus Christ. It's my hope that throughout the experiences we'll have today, we'll seek to understand the light of his life.

Lead the group in prayer, asking Jesus to join the study today and to give everyone wisdom to discern between New Age ideas and true spirituality. Turn on the lights, blow out the large candle, and set it aside to use later.

Leader tip

Even though the markers are not permanent, have people place strips of tape on the part of the face they want to change and then draw on the tape whatever feature they're trying to create.

■ Changing Faces

(25 to 30 minutes)

Supplies: Bibles, paper, masking tape, yarn, assorted nonpermanent markers

Have students form trios, and have each person tell about one famous, historical person he or she admires and why.

While they're talking, give each trio a roll of masking tape, paper, yarn, and an assortment of colored, nonpermanent markers. Say: **To begin our study of true spiritual growth, we're going to get some hands-on experience in becoming like someone we admire. During the next several minutes, you're going to decorate the faces of your**

True or False Spirituality

The New Age movement is a loosely connected assortment of beliefs about the nature of life, humanity, and eternity. Although the beliefs often seem to contradict each other, they all share a common "root" belief: that humans are capable of attaining "godhood" or are, in fact, already "gods." Here's a sampling of some of those New Age beliefs, as explained in *The Seduction of Our Children,* by Neil T. Anderson and Steve Russo:

✂ -

This is what it means to be spiritual: *God is everything, and everything is God.* Everything in creation—trees, snails, books, people, earthworms—are one divine essence. The more we are attuned to that consciousness, the more we are God.

✂ -

This is what it means to be spiritual: *We must become cosmically conscious.* We become self-realized through reincarnation, where our souls progress through many life cycles until we become fully conscious of the universe.

✂ -

This is what it means to be spiritual: *We must work together toward the harmony of a one-world government.* A new global civilization and a mystic world religion is necessary to unite all people in a worldwide consciousness and create world peace.

✂ -

This is what it means to be spiritual: *What you believe to be good is good, and what you believe to be evil is evil.* Reality is what you make it. By changing what you believe, you can change reality.

✂ -

trio members to help each person look something like the person he or she admires.

Tell students to use the supplies creatively to make their partners resemble the people they admire. For example, if Jeff says he admires Abraham Lincoln, his partners can use the supplies to make a yarn "beard" for Jeff and then use tape to give him a bigger nose or chin.

When trios are ready, have them introduce their "celebrity make overs" to the whole group. Have students give awards for "Best Make Over," "Most Famous-Looking," or "Most Creative Use of Tape."

Tell people they can remove the tape from their faces; then ask everyone to get a Bible. Still in their trios, have people open their Bibles to Psalm 1 and Galatians 5:16-26. Then say: **Read these verses in your trios, and look for how these passages describe true spirituality and spiritual growth.**

After trios have read both passages, have them discuss these questions:

● **What do these Scriptures say about true spirituality and spiritual growth?**

● **Based on these, what does someone spiritual "look like"?**

● **Do you know anyone with those attributes? Explain.**

Leader tip

Because of the fun and excitement of this activity, people will probably quickly lose the "reflective" mood created at the opening of the study. That's OK. Later when you're ready to guide them back into a reflective mode, they'll remember the opening and be able to make the transition much more easily.

Biblical Background

One misconception people often struggle with is that spiritual character as it's described in Galatians 5:16-26 is the result of human effort and commitment. The Apostle Paul, however, called these character qualities the "fruit of the Spirit," indicating that these inner qualities result from the Holy Spirit's working within the heart of the Christian. The fruit of the Spirit isn't something we can manufacture or do ourselves—it's the natural outgrowth of an intimate relationship with God.

Leader tip

Most trios will decorate a person to "look like" Jesus. If they don't, ask them to compare their person's qualities with the qualities described in Psalm 1 and Galatians 5:16-26. Then read aloud John 1:1-5, and ask:

● Who does this passage describe?

● Why is Jesus the "light"?

Say: **Now use the supplies again to make one person in your trio "look like" a famous, historical person that garnered those attributes.** If students have trouble, suggest that to make someone look loving, they tape a heart shape to his or her chest. Or to make someone look strong, they create big muscles to tape onto his or her arms. Tell students they can decorate the person's whole body—carefully. When trios finish, have them present their "make overs" to everyone and explain both why they chose that person and why they decorated their trio members as they did.

Ask:

● **How did the focus change from the first make over to the second?**

● **How is that new focus similar to what we have to focus on to grow spiritually?**

Say: **Jesus Christ is our ultimate example of how to live. In becoming more like Jesus, we grow spiritually. Most people in the New Age movement believe that through meditation or spiritual experiences, they can become like gods.** Ask:

● **Is our desire to become like Jesus (who is God) the same thing? Why or why not?**

● **How do New Age practitioners try to become like "gods"?**

● **How do Christians try to become like Jesus?**

● **What's the difference between New Age spirituality and true spiritual growth?**

Say: **Real spiritual growth doesn't happen by our own efforts. But as we make our relationship with Jesus the priority in our lives, he changes us to become more and more like him. That's real spiritual growth. So the question is: How do we make our relationship with Jesus a priority? Let's try to answer that question together.**

■ Personal Evaluation

(10 to 15 minutes)

Supplies: A large candle, a matchbook, tea-light candles, "Jesus and Me" handouts (p. 105), pencils, newsprint, tape, a marker

Have students get back into the circle of chairs from the beginning of the study (be sure a chair is still in the center of the circle). Say: **Think of the best friend you've ever had—or would like to have. Imagine that person sitting in this chair. What kinds of things would you do to build trust in each other and grow closer together as friends?**

Write people's responses on newsprint, and tape it to a wall.

Once you have five to ten specific responses, relight the "Jesus candle" and place it on the chair in the center of the circle. Turn off the lights, and say: **Now, instead of your best earthly friend, imagine that Jesus is sitting in this chair. Our goal is to grow spiritually by becoming more like him—and by making him our best friend of all.**

Give each person a tea-light candle, and have everyone light his or her candle from the Jesus candle. When all the candles are lit, say: **Your lighted candles represent Jesus being with you wherever you go. He is with you as a true friend and constant companion, eager to help you become more like him as you get to know him better.**

Instruct each person to select one item from the list of ways to grow closer to a friend. As students are making their choices, distribute the "Jesus and Me" handouts and pencils. Then have each person move to a place to be alone and spend a few moments getting to know Jesus better, guided by the questions on the handout.

Allow people up to ten minutes to complete their handouts. When time is up, call everyone back to the circle. Leave the lights off, and have people keep their candles burning, along with the Jesus candle in the center of the circle. Ask for volunteers to tell what they discovered or experienced in this activity. After several people have shared, say: **Spiritual growth—true spirituality—means becoming more like Jesus. And as many of us have just discovered, we don't have to do it by ourselves. Jesus wants to know us and help us grow to be more like him.**

Leader tip

Students' experiences in this activity may differ widely. Some may have an intimate experience with God, while others may become bored or anxious. As people share their private experiences, encourage them to be honest—even if the experience wasn't great. Then ask:

● Why do you think our experiences weren't the same just now?

● What does that tell you about the way Jesus builds a relationship with each of us?

● What can you do to make your next experience with Jesus even more positive than this one?

■ Group Building

(5 to 10 minutes)

Supplies: Tea-light candles

Have students turn their chairs so that each person is facing a partner and so two candles are burning between each pair.

Say: **Becoming like Jesus doesn't happen in a vacuum because he often reveals himself through the people around us. We can grow spiritually by learning more about each other.**

Leader tip

During the time of silent eye contact, some people may become uncomfortable and laugh or talk. As you see this happen, gently encourage those pairs to maintain eye contact and remain silent for the full minute.

Instruct the pairs to maintain silent eye contact for one minute as they think about the Christlike character qualities they see in each other's lives. When time is up, have pairs maintain eye contact while they tell their partners what qualities of Jesus they see in them. For example, Tony might say to Bill, "I appreciate the love and kindness you show people. You seem to have a genuine respect for others, just as Jesus did."

Once partners have shared, have them pray together, asking Jesus to help them both become more like him. As people finish their prayers, encourage them to keep their candles this week as reminders of Jesus' presence.

"But the fruit of the Spirit is love, joy, peace, patience, kindness, goodness, faithfulness, gentleness and self-control. Against such things there is no law. Those who belong to Christ Jesus have crucified the sinful nature with its passions and desires. Since we live by the Spirit, let us keep in step with the Spirit."

–Galatians 5:22-25

Jesus and Me
handout

Set your candle in front of you and pray for Jesus to help you grow spiritually. Here's an example:

Jesus, I want you to come and be with me now. I want to know you better, so I can become more like you. Please show me how to grow spiritually.

As you continue in an attitude of prayer, write your responses to these questions:

1. Do you believe Jesus is with you right now? Why or why not?

2. What are three things you can do to become more aware of Jesus' presence in your life?

3. If you were to let Jesus help you grow spiritually over the next month, what do you think would change about your life?

4. Does the thought of those changes excite you or frighten you? Why?

5. Do you think the Scripture to the right is true? Why or why not?

   "Blessed is the man...[whose] delight is in the law of the Lord, and on his law he meditate[s] day and night. He is like a tree planted by streams of water, which yields its fruit in season and whose leaf does not wither. Whatever he does prospers"
   (Psalm 1:1-3).

6. What will you do about this passage this week?

Looking Out

looking out

Families in Intensive Care

Fitting In

How to Talk With Others About God

If You Love Me, You'll...

Mentor Me!

Reality Bites

Families in Intensive Care

How God's Forgiveness Can Heal Families

BIBLICAL POINT: God can heal your family.

BIBLE BASIS: Genesis 37:1-28; 45:1-15

TOPIC: Family

The robed minister led the congregation in the Lord's Prayer. "Our Friend, who art in heaven…" they said together, heads bowed.

Huh? *"Friend?"*

"I no longer refer to God as 'Father,'" explained the minister later. "So many people have suffered pain in their families, and fathers are often not considered loving."

Fathers. Mothers. Brothers and sisters. The people who know us best have the power to bruise us most easily. A cutting word, a broken promise, or a simple lack of attention can cause us pain that goes straight to the heart. Over time, the offenses meld into an overwhelming list of grievances that distort our view of family.

As young adults seek more independence and separate themselves from their families, conflict intensifies. While your group members may think the solution to family conflict and bad history lies in distancing themselves emotionally, they'll soon realize that the pain doesn't just disappear. But there's hope for healing, and this study will help students discover where to find it.

Through examining the story of Joseph's family, students can learn that God's forgiveness can bring complete healing to families.

Before the study, gather together the following supplies:

- Bibles,
- index cards,
- pencils,
- paper towels,
- markers, and
- self-stick notes.

families in intensive care

● God can heal your family.

■ Hi, Honey! I'm Home!

(15 to 20 minutes)

Supplies: Index cards, pencils

As students arrive, hand each one an index card and a pencil. Say: **Today we're going to talk about our families. Write on your card the television family that most closely resembles your own family. You can choose any family from past or present TV shows. After you've identified a family, write a sentence or two explaining why that family resembles yours. *Don't* write your name on your card because we're all going to try to guess the families described on the cards.**

When everyone has finished, collect and shuffle the cards. Distribute one card to each student; then have each student read aloud what's written on the card. After each student reads, have everyone guess whose family is described on the card.

Say: **We've just taken a fun look at our families, but sometimes our families give us a lot of frustration and grief. Often our parents and siblings have the greatest potential to hurt us because we expect them to love and support us no matter what. Today we'll explore how God can heal your family. We'll begin by examining a family that would make a great soap opera family.**

Family Abuse

As you discuss family hurts with your students, someone may reveal that a parent or sibling has been abusive. If a student makes such a revelation, you may have legal responsibilities—depending on the student's age—to notify Child Protection Services or other agencies that will address the situation. To determine your legal duties as mandated in your state, contact the Child Help National Child Abuse Hotline at 800-422-4453. You might also wish to develop a church policy for handling this type of situation.

Never trivialize the effects of abuse, even if a student is a legal adult or if the abuse ended years ago. Always offer support and prayer through the student's recovery.

Another possibility is that a student will confess to abusing a sibling or other family member. Again, be aware of a possible legal responsibility to report the abuse. Also, help the student accept God's healing forgiveness, and offer prayer and support through the student's recovery.

■ Biblical Family Exploration

(30 to 35 minutes)

Supplies: Bibles, paper towels, markers, self-stick notes

Hand each student a paper towel. Say: **Being in a family can be a lot like playing football. There are hits and tackles, setbacks and advances. But football has an advantage—referees. When something unfair happens, referees throw their flags and blow their whistles. Then** they turn to the stands, explain the foul, and proclaim a penalty for the offending team. Once that happens, it's over. The game goes on.

Maybe families could use referees. As we look in the Bible at Joseph's family, we're going to adopt the role of referee. I'm going to read the story of Joseph's family. As I do, listen for "family fouls"—the ways Joseph's family members hurt each other. When you hear an "infraction," whistle and throw your "flag." We'll stop the "action," and then we'll attempt to learn from Joseph's and his brothers' mistakes.

Read aloud Genesis 37:1-28. Stop reading whenever someone throws a flag. Have whoever throws a flag explain the foul he or she noticed. Then write the infraction on a self-stick note, and stick the note to a wall. Once people have fully discussed that foul, resume reading until someone else throws a flag.

After you've finished reading Joseph's story, you'll have a collection of self-stick notes on the wall. Say: **As we look at the infractions on this "wall of shame," we realize that Joseph's family needed major work to get beyond their hurts.**

Have each student turn to a partner to discuss these questions (encourage pairs to get up and look at the self-stick notes if they need to):

● **Do you relate to anything written on the self-stick notes? If so, what and why?**

● **What kinds of family fouls have occurred in your family?**

● **What's been your usual reaction to those fouls?**

● **What could Joseph or his brothers have done to reconcile their family fouls?**

● **Would you like your family fouls to be reconciled? Why?**

● **What could your role be in reconciling the issues that cause your family's fouls?**

● **How can God heal your family?**

When pairs have finished their discussions, have them read Genesis 45:1-15. Ask:

● **In this passage, what did Joseph, his brothers, and God do about the family's pain?**

● **Do you think God healed Joseph's family? Why or why not?**

Say: **Joseph had a prime opportunity to exact justice in this passage. He could have evened the score in the game, making his brothers pay penalties for all the family fouls they'd committed against him. Joseph could have let his brothers go hungry or even imprisoned them. Instead he chose to forgive them, and because he did, God healed his family. To represent this, let's remove all the notes from the wall.** Have students help you remove the self-stick notes, tear them up, and throw them away.

Hand each student a marker, and say: **This wall of shame is now clean. Think of what your family's wall of shame looks like right now. On your paper-towel penalty flag, write a list of offenses and hurts that would appear on your family's wall of shame.**

When people have finished writing their lists, say: **Look at your lists. Remember that God healed Joseph's family when Joseph chose to forgive his family members.**

Have everyone turn to a partner to discuss these questions:

● **As you look at your list, do you think God can heal your family through forgiveness? Why or why not?**

● **Based on the story of Joseph, what do you think true forgiveness looks like?**

● **Who do you need to forgive?**

● **How would you go about forgiving that person?**

● **Who do you need to ask to forgive you?**

● **How would you go about asking that person to forgive you?**

● **What's one thing you'll do this week to clear your family's wall of shame?**

● **What results do you expect from forgiveness? Are they realistic?**

Have each student tell his or her partner one quality the partner has that will help clear that family's wall of shame. For example, someone might say, "You're a good listener, and God can use your listening skills to heal your family."

Say: **God can heal your family as you and your family members choose to forgive each other. Keep your penalty flag to remind you to seek forgiveness for your family fouls. As you forgive others and**

Understanding Forgiveness

When you tell people that they need to forgive those who've hurt them, they'll probably say, "Yeah, right. There's no way I'm going to forgive that person. If I do, he (or she) will just walk all over me again."

But forgiveness and trust are two different issues. God commands that we forgive others. In Matthew 6:14-15, Jesus says, "For if you forgive men when they sin against you, your heavenly Father will also forgive you. But if you do not forgive men their sins, your Father will not forgive your sins." Forgiving others allows God's forgiveness to flow to us. And not only does it free the person we forgive, it frees us from expecting a payback. We can release the situation and move on. This happens even if the person who hurt us doesn't apologize for what he or she did.

But forgiving someone doesn't mean that we automatically extend trust to that person again. It's natural and healthy to question the relationship and to refrain from relying on that person again until he or she can prove trustworthy. This doesn't mean we hold the original offense over this person's head. Instead, it means waiting until that person builds trust in little things before trusting him or her in bigger things. This may never happen, especially if this person thinks he or she never did anything wrong.

So when students express dismay about forgiving others, help them understand the distinction between forgiveness and trust. This explanation will help them free themselves from past hurts and move forward with their lives.

ask others to forgive you, mark off the situations that have been "cleared" from your family's wall of shame. When you've addressed all of the family fouls, throw your penalty flag away.

■ Forgive Me...I Forgive...

(5 to 10 minutes)
Supplies: None needed

Dim the lights, and have each student find a place away from everyone else. Say: **Get into a comfortable position. I'm going to lead us in a prayer time. In the Lord's Prayer, Jesus teaches us to pray 'Forgive us our debts, as we also have forgiven our debtors'** (Matthew 6:12). **We're going to pray a similar prayer. I'll pray aloud, raising topics for us to discuss with God. After each topic, I'll pause for a few seconds to allow you to pray silently about that issue.**

Pray: **Dear God, we thank you for Jesus, who died to save us from the consequences of our sins. Right now, we confess all our sins to you. We confess to you those sins we've committed in action.** Pause for fifteen seconds, and then pray: **We confess those sins we've committed in attitude.** Pause for fifteen seconds, and then pray: **We confess sins we've committed in our secret thought life.** Pause for fifteen seconds, and then pray: **And we confess sins of not doing what you've called us to do.** Pause for fifteen seconds, and then pray: **We don't deserve your forgiveness. We've done nothing to earn it, but we ask for you to forgive us for our part in putting your Son to death on the Cross.** Pause for fifteen seconds, and then pray: **We also ask you to forgive us for our part in our families' hurts.** Pause for fifteen seconds, and then pray: **Thank you, Father. We feel the weight of our sin lifting as your grace floods our souls.**

Now, Lord, we ask for your grace to flow through us to our families. We ask you to help us forgive those who've hurt us by accident, intent, or neglect. Pause for fifteen seconds, and then pray: **Help us show your love to others, Lord.** Pause for fifteen seconds, and then pray: **We pray in the name of Jesus. Amen.**

Biblical Background

God's forgiveness makes it possible for our families to heal from the hurts we inflict on each other. To further empower your students to implement healing in their families, encourage them to study the following biblical passages:

- Psalm 130—God forgives us for our sins.
- Matthew 18:21-35—Jesus says that we must forgive people again and again and that God will forgive us as we forgive others.
- Mark 2:1-12—Jesus forgives a paralyzed man and then heals him.
- Luke 19:1-9—Jesus forgives Zacchaeus.
- John 21:15-19—Jesus symbolically forgives Peter for denying him.
- Acts 2:38-39—Peter proclaims the forgiveness of sins through Jesus' death and resurrection.

Understanding Families

Many family counselors view families as systems—groupings of unique and important people who unite to create a whole and original entity. Just as a car is a system with each part relying on the others to make the car run, each family member's behavior affects how everyone else acts to make the family function. For example, if Elizabeth yells at her mom, her mom might yell back, her stepbrother might withdraw, and her stepdad might attempt to mediate the conflict.

According to family systems theory, when one family member changes how he or she usually acts in certain situations, the system reacts in one of two ways—attempts to squelch the changes in that one person to maintain the accustomed balance or changes to achieve a new way of interacting. For example, if Elizabeth usually yells at her mom but instead chooses to walk away from the conflict, her mom might either yell at her to encourage Elizabeth's usual reaction, or her mom might give Elizabeth some space and then calmly approach her later.

This systems view partly explains why families with young adults may experience increased chaos. As young adults mature and gain more independence, the rest of the family has to adjust. Some family members don't want to adjust—they'd rather things remain the same. Others want to accommodate the changes but don't know how. In addition, most families with young adults must also accommodate parents in midlife, also a tough life passage. These forces combine to push even the most healthy family out of kilter.

Family systems theory can also help students understand how God can use them to heal their families' hurts. As students react differently to their family members, everyone else must adjust. As students offer forgiveness instead of bitterness to parents, stepparents, siblings, and stepsiblings, these family members can also change their behavior. The positive change of one person forgiving another can help families out of deep, dark holes of discouragement, despair, bitterness, and frustration.

Fitting In

Building Friendships in the Church

BIBLICAL POINT: You're important to the church.
BIBLE BASIS: Exodus 35:30–36:2; 37:1-9; 39:43; and 1 Corinthians 12:7, 27
TOPIC: Belonging

Most young adults haven't established homes. Most haven't established long-term careers. Most haven't established families. But they're no longer considered part of their parents' homes, careers, or families. They're on their own, and they don't belong to anyone. They're searching for intimacy and a sense of community.

They can find it in the body of Christ.

This study sends people on a series of investigations to discover their God-given talents and how those abilities can be used to help others. Through these investigations, group members can learn that they're important to the church—and that the church can bring a true sense of belonging to their lives.

Before the study, gather together the following supplies:
● Bibles,
● markers,
● scissors,
● tape,
● safety pins or tape,
● colored paper, and
● rubber bands.

■ Your Gift

(15 to 20 minutes)

Supplies: A Bible, colored paper, safety pins or tape

Once everyone has arrived, read 1 Corinthians 12:27 aloud. Then say:
1 Corinthians 12:27 tells us that all Christians make up the body of Christ, which is the church. And each of us has a specific part to play in the church. To play our part, we all have special gifts and talents.

Have students form pairs and think of a special ability or gift their partners have that helps others—for example, "Your smile uplifts people" or "You're really good at encouraging others when they're down."

fitting in
● You're important to the church.

When pairs finish, say: **Now that you've thought of a gift or talent your partner has, make a symbol of that special ability.**

Have each partner tear colored paper to make some kind of badge to represent the other partner's talent. For example, if one person's gift is encouragement, his or her partner could tear paper into a heart shape.

As people finish, have them pin or tape the symbols they created to their partners' shirts. Then let the people wander around the room for half a minute or so to admire one another's badges.

Read 1 Corinthians 12:7 aloud. Then say: **1 Corinthians 12:7 tells us that although we're all given gifts when we become Christians, our gifts are not for ourselves. They're to be used to help others.** Have people find new partners; then have them try to "give" their gifts to their partners. For example, if someone's special gift is a "great smile," have him or her smile at the partner. Or if someone's gift is mercy or compassion, have that person offer to pray right then for his or her partner's needs.

After a few minutes, have pairs discuss the following questions:

● **How did you feel when you tried to share your gift with your partner? Explain.**

● **How is that like the way it might feel in real life for you to use your gifts in the church?**

● **How does it make you feel, knowing that God has given you gifts to use in the church? Explain.**

● **Why do you think God gives every Christian gifts?**

Say: **Today we're going to investigate how your role in God's church can change people's lives and help you build deep, lasting friendships.**

Before we dive into our next investigation, let's ask God to help us grasp the truths he wants us to understand.

In the same pairs, have students take turns praying for each other. First, have them thank God for their partners' talents or gifts. Then have them ask God to help them understand his Word and apply it to their lives.

■ Using the Gifts We're Given

(30 to 35 minutes)

Supplies: Bibles, markers, scissors, tape, safety pins, colored paper

Say: **We've seen at least one ability each of you has that can help others. Having that ability makes you important to the people around you and to this church. God has placed you here because there's a need for what you have to offer. Now, let's look at a person from the Bible named Bezalel** (BEZ-uh-lel). **Beyond natural abilities, he was given specific gifts from God to perform special duties for God's people.**

Have students form three groups, and assign each group a set of these passages:

● Exodus 35:30–36:2;
● Exodus 37:1-9; and
● Exodus 39:43 and 1 Corinthians 12:7.

Talents vs. Gifts

Each of us has talents or abilities. And if we're Christians, each of us has gifts from the Holy Spirit, too. So what's the difference?

Spiritual gifts are "supernaturally" based. That means they're abilities the Holy Spirit has bestowed on Christians to serve God's people. They are not natural abilities. For this reason, natural talents such as a good singing voice or athleticism are not spiritual gifts, even though they can be used powerfully to serve God.

1 Corinthians 12:8-10 provides a partial list of gifts the Holy Spirit gives. Some examples of the Holy Spirit's gifts include wisdom, knowledge, and faith.

Whatever combination of talents and gifts your group members have, they can be encouraged to know that they can use all their gifts "in concert" to serve God and the church if they submit their gifts to the will of God's Holy Spirit.

Within their groups, have students assign people these roles:
● Reader—reads the Scriptures,
● Checker—make sure everyone understands, and
● Timekeeper—makes sure the group completes its task within ten minutes.

Set out the same supplies you used in the "Your Gift" activity. Then say: **Your group's task is to study your assigned Scripture passage and then teach everyone what you've learned. To do that, study your passage and then choose an object or idea from the passage to re-create using the supplies I've provided. For example, you might make a symbol to represent wisdom, a model of a craftsman, or even an ark. Once you've created your object, your entire group must use it to explain your passage to everyone. You have ten minutes.**

After ten minutes, have groups make their presentations using the objects they created. Then have students find partners to discuss these questions:

● **How did using the object you created help you explain your passage?**

● **How is creating an object to teach others similar to using your gifts and abilities to help others in the church? How is it different?**

● **How does using your gifts for others help build or deepen your friendships?**

● **How are you like Bezalel? different?**

● **Do you think Bezalel felt like he fit in? Why or why not?**

● **Do you feel like you fit in with God's people? Why or why not?**

● **How does knowing that you're important to the church affect how much you feel like you "belong" here?**

● **What can you do this week to use your gifts and abilities to help build deeper friendships with others in the church?**

Say: **Bezalel was not a pastor or a priest, but the talent God gave him was important to God's people. In the same way, you're important to the church. We belong to each other. And as we learn to use our gifts and abilities to serve each other, we'll build deep, lasting friendships.**

■ Connections

(5 to 10 minutes)

Supplies: Rubber bands, scissors

Give everyone a rubber band. If possible, have rubber bands of various sizes and colors to signify the differences among peoples' gifts. Have students string their rubber bands together by looping one rubber band around another and pulling it back through itself.

Once all the rubber bands have been connected, have two students hold each end and stretch the rubber bands out. Have the other students stand with you near the middle of the strand.

Say: **The church is like this long string of rubber bands. We all need each other and are given gifts from God to help each other. When we're using our gifts, we're all connected and can feel like we belong. But if someone won't use his or her gift, it's bad for all of us.**

Using a pair of scissors, hold onto one of the rubber bands and cut it out of the strand. Ask:

● **How is what happened to this rubber band chain like what happens when people don't use their gifts in the church?**

● **What can we do to prevent that from happening?**

Close by saying: **You're important to the church. Pray this week that God will continue to show you how the gifts he has given you can help you to build deep friendships within the church.**

Testing Gifts

Your students may wonder, "How do I know if my gifts truly are from God?" 1 Corinthians 12:3 provides a good test. It says, "Therefore I tell you that no one who is speaking by the Spirit of God says, 'Jesus be cursed,' and no one can say, 'Jesus is Lord,' except by the Holy Spirit." So people who bring glory to Jesus with their gifts can be assured that their gifts are from God.

Other verses in the Bible that also show us how to test the gifts include Matthew 7:15-20 (which tells us to look for "fruit") and Romans 8:9 (which instructs us to question whether a person is controlled by the Holy Spirit or a sinful nature).

How to Talk With Others About God

BIBLICAL POINT: You have to know your story before you can share it.

BIBLE BASIS: 2 Kings 22:1–23:30 and Philippians 3:2-11

TOPIC: Sharing Faith

Let's say a visitor walks into your meeting, but instead of a normal greeting like "What's up?" or "How's it goin'?" he says, "What's your story? Why are you really here?" What would your group members say? Do they have stories to tell about their relationships with God? And if they do, do they know how to tell them?

What if one of your group members spoke out and said: "My story is about grace—how much I've needed it and how often God has offered it to me. My story is about trying to make life work on my own, but ending up lost, isolated, lonely, and afraid. And my story is about how, in the middle of that darkness, God loved me and offered to be the co-author of my life. Now I'm learning that God doesn't want to write my story for *me*—he wants to write it *with me*. And as we create together, I'm learning that my story can actually offer hope and truth to others. That's my story. Would you like to hear more?"

Each of your group members has a story to tell—one that God has helped write. Others need to hear those stories—people who need hope but can't find it. This study will help students find God's grace in their stories and then tell their stories to those around them.

Before the study, move the furniture to the sides of your meeting room and cover the floor in newsprint; or use roll ends from a printer for ease (you may want to tape the newsprint to the floor in spots to keep it from shifting). Gather together

- colored markers,
- pens,
- old magazines,
- glue, and
- scissors.

how to talk with others about God

- You have to know your story before you can share it.

Pile those supplies together in the center of the room.
You'll also need

● Bibles,
● one "Tell Me a Story" handout (p. 124) for every two people, and
● tape.

■ Room Transformation

(10 to 15 minutes)

Supplies: Colored markers, pens, old magazines, glue, scissors, newsprint

As people enter the meeting room, have them remove their shoes. Then have people scatter around the room and each create his or her own "personal space" on the floor by drawing a shape (a circle, square, letter outline, or whatever) on the newsprint you prepared before the study. The shape should be big enough to sit in. Ask students to decorate their shapes however they'd like (point them to the supply pile for decoration ideas).

When people finish, have them form groups of three with people whose shapes are located close to theirs. Have trios draw a circle in the space between their three shapes and then sit down around the circle.

Say: **Show your two partners your personal space design; then draw a pathway from your shapes to the circle you just created.**

Once trios finish this task, have them think about what their partners' personal-space design says about them. Say: **Inside the pathway that leads from your personal space to the trio circle, write an ending for the following statement for each of your partners: "(Name), based on how you've decorated your personal space, I think you're a person who..."**

When trios are finished, say: **Now look at what your group members wrote about you. Tell them whether they're right or wrong about you, and why.**

After a few minutes, ask students to tell what they learned about their group members. Then ask:

● **How did it feel to have others draw conclusions about you with very little information?**

● **How did it feel when they were right? wrong?**

● **How did you feel when you gave someone in your group feedback and that person disagreed with your conclusions? agreed?**

● **How are all these feelings like the way you feel when you're relating with people at school, home, work, or church?**

Say: **Tell your partners something you'd like them to know about you. When you're finished, write in the circle one thing you liked about what your partners shared.**

Then say: **Each of us has a story to tell about who we are. Often the people around us—even our closest friends—don't understand us because we're not always very good at telling our own stories. Today we'll investigate our own stories and the stories of the** people around us. We'll explore how God has been the "co-author" in our lives to this point, and we'll learn how we can help others by sharing God's impact on our lives.

■ Personal Investigation

(15 to 20 minutes)

Supplies: Pens, markers, "Tell Me a Story" handouts (p. 124), newsprint, tape

Ask students to form new pairs with someone not in their trios. Have pairs draw a pathway between their personal spaces. Then give each pair a copy of the "Tell Me a Story" handout, and say: **Pick one of the choices on the handout, and share it with your partner.**

After pairs have shared, say: **Now that you've each heard your partner tell a story that affected him or her, write in the pathway between your shapes at least two things that positively affected you about your partner's story. Don't forget to write *why* you were influenced. You have two minutes.**

While people are working, write the list of bulleted suggestions below on newsprint, and tape the newsprint to a wall. Feel free to add to this list if you think of other ideas.

When people finish writing, ask them to share what they've written with their partners. Then say: **The next journaling experience will be more personal. Inside your personal space, write a short story about God's influence in your life. For example, you could write about a time when...**

- **things seemed bleak, but God somehow gave you hope.**
- **you were surprised by a desire to know who God is, and you were drawn to pursuing some kind of relationship with him.**
- **you were hurt and confused because God didn't act the way you expected him to.**
- **you felt close to God.**
- **you felt far away from God.**
- **you felt like standing up for God.**
- **you felt like you really needed God in your life.**

After a few minutes, say: **Now I'd like you to talk to your partner about what you wrote. Be sure you tell your partner something you learned about yourself because of this life experience.**

After partners share, have them discuss these questions:

- **Was it easy to think of some way God has impacted your story? Why or why not?**
- **What's most difficult about telling someone else about God's impact on your life?**
- **If your friends outside of this group knew about God's impact on you, how would that affect them?**
- **What does it mean to "share your faith" with someone?**

Say: **Even though God has been a co-author of our stories, it's**

Leader tip

What about students who say they're Christians but have no evident relationship with Christ? If people claim that God has no impact on their lives, consider calling them aside and *lovingly* confronting them with these difficult questions:

- **What does being a Christian mean to you?**
- **The Bible teaches that being a Christian means receiving God's forgiveness for our sins and then following Jesus every day. Do you think this is true? Why or why not?**
- **If what the Bible teaches *is* true, why would it be important for a follower of Jesus to have an ongoing daily relationship with him?**
- **Do you want an ongoing daily relationship with Jesus? Why or why not?**

If people express interest in a personal relationship with Jesus, pray with them right there, asking God to guide them into a personal relationship with him.

easy to "edit out" his impact on us when we're telling our stories to others. That's why it's important to be prepared to talk with others about God's role in our lives. You have to know your story before you can share it. To discover more about how to share our stories, let's explore how God deeply impacted the stories of two men—and what happened because of it.

■ Bible Investigation

(15 to 20 minutes)

Supplies: Bibles, newsprint, tape, markers

At one end of your meeting area, draw a circle on the newsprint, and write the name "Josiah" in the circle. At the other end of the meeting area, draw a circle on the newsprint and write the name "Paul" in the circle. Then say: **Imagine that one day, a lot of children will be a part of your story. Imagine that you and your spouse are pregnant with a son and that you have just these two names to choose from. Which one would you pick to name your son? Once you decide, draw a pathway to the circle that represents your choice, and sit near it.**

Once people have gathered by the two circles, give each group a Bible, and ask each group to choose a reader. Then say: **In a moment I'll assign each reader a biblical passage to read aloud. As you listen to the passage, think about how you'd answer these two questions: How did God impact this person's story? Why did this person respond to God the way he did?**

Tell the Josiah-group reader to read aloud 2 Kings 22:1–23:30. Have the Paul-group reader read aloud Philippians 3:2-11. While the readers are reading, write the two questions on newsprint, and tape the newsprint to a wall.

When both readers finish, have groups discuss the two questions you wrote on the newsprint. Then have each group appoint a reporter to tell everyone what the group learned about its biblical character. After the reporters share, say: **I'd like to add one more story to those we've been studying—it's my story.**

Tell your group members your own story of how God has changed your life. Then call everyone together, and ask:

● **How have these stories—mine, Josiah's, and Paul's—affected you?**

● **What does that say about how your story can influence others for Christ?**

Have students look around the room at the newsprint "network" they've created. Ask:

● **How is creating these pathways on the newsprint like sharing our stories with others in real life?**

● **What would happen to you if you never shared your story with anyone?**

Biblical Background

Josiah stands out in Old Testament history as a passionate reformer and humble leader who, as king of Judah, tried to lead his people into repentance for their idol worship and cavalier attitude toward God.

Josiah began his journey as a leader when he was only eight years old. Before he became king, Judah had grown corrupt with foreign, idolatrous influences. For more than fifty years, idol worship had replaced the law of Moses, and immorality was rampant. In fact, the people of Judah so ignored God in their daily lives that Josiah didn't even know what God expected of his people. When workers restoring the Temple in Jerusalem discovered a copy of God's laws, Josiah read them and grieved that the people had strayed so far from God's design for them.

When Josiah was just sixteen, he stopped practicing the traditional idol worship of the people and searched for ways to honor God in his life. Then when he was twenty, he decided to vigorously purge idolatry from Judah. He ordered altars, statues, and icons of pagan gods destroyed. He banished prostitutes from the temple, banned child sacrifices, and removed idolatrous religious leaders from office. At the same time, he repopularized the reading of God's laws and personally pledged to follow them with all his heart.

When he was thirty-nine, Josiah was killed in battle fighting the Egyptians. And soon after, Judah returned to idol worship.

■ Share Your Story

(5 to 10 minutes)

Supplies: Colored markers, pens

Say: **We've begun to see God's impact on others' stories and our own. But how can we let others know the good news, that God loves us and wants to be a co-author with us in creating our life stories? In your personal space, I'd like you to create a symbol or drawing that represents God's impact on your life's story. Then we'll discuss ways you can use your symbol or drawing to tell your story. But before we begin, let's ask our co-author to help us share our stories with the people around us.**

Open the prayer time by asking God to show group members how he has affected their lives. Then invite people to express their own prayers to God, either silently or aloud.

After the prayer time, pile colored markers in the center of the room for people to use in creating their symbol. When people finish, have two or three students explain their symbols' meanings to the group.

Then say: **To close, I'd like each of you to tear your symbol out of your personal space and then write on the back one way you can use your symbol to tell others about God's impact on your life.**

When people are finished, say: **I challenge you to follow through with your idea this week. Now that you know something of your story, you can share it with others!**

Tell Me a Story

handout

- Tell a favorite childhood story.

- Tell a story about the greatest thing that's ever happened to you.

- Pick out something in this room that reveals something about your story, and then explain why.

- Pick the one person in the world whose life story most attracts you. Explain why that person's life interests you.

- Tell a story about an event in your life that wasn't easy but that changed you for the better.

If You Love Me, You'll...

Loving Without Conditions

BIBLICAL POINT: Real love is a free gift.

BIBLE BASIS: 1 Samuel 20 and 1 Corinthians 13:4-7

TOPIC: Love

Unconditional love is just an illusion. There are no free lunches here. No free rides. This is the land of "you scratch my back, and I'll scratch yours." It's called the law of give and take, and it rules this world. Everything has a price—from sneakers to education to the love of a gang. All you need to know is the cost. All you need to do is pay it. That is, if you can...

They've been called the Bottom-Line Generation, and for good reason. Your students have learned to survive in a world where everything comes with a cost. Nothing is free—especially the things that really matter, such as friendship, belonging, and love.

With their wizened, you-don't-get-something-for-nothing attitude, the very idea of "unconditional love" can sound ludicrous to today's young adults. They might even call it dysfunctional.

This study guides people to discover that unconditional love is real. It's theirs to receive from the One who loves them most, and theirs to give to each other and a hurting world.

Before the study, gather together the following supplies:
- Bibles,
- heavy aluminum foil,
- permanent markers,
- streamers,
- tape,
- magazines,
- a cassette or CD player, and
- a cassette or CD.

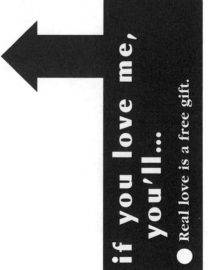

if you love me, you'll...
● Real love is a free gift.

■ Arms of Love

(5 to 10 minutes)

Supplies: None needed

Have people form a circle; then have them number off by twos. Say: **Today we're going to talk about real and false love. You're going to discover how you can tell whether somebody who says, "I love you" really means it. To get us started, I want all the Ones to place your arms around the shoulders of the Twos on either side of you.**

Once students are in position, have them remain that way throughout the following discussion time. Ask:

● **Do you feel like you know what love is? Why or why not?**

● **Have you ever believed someone loved you—only to discover he or she really didn't? Explain.**

● **How would you know if someone who claimed to love you really didn't?**

● **Have you ever felt that you wouldn't be loved by someone unless you did what he or she wanted? Explain.**

● **Do you think people who withhold love that way really love you? Why or why not?**

Say: **People in real life sometimes attach "price tags" to their love. They require you to do things to "earn" their affection, or they withhold love until you behave the way they want you to. These relationships may seem like they're based on love, but they're really not. That's because real love is always a free gift.**

Ask the Ones:

● **How does it feel to be giving a "free gift" of love to the people around you right now? Explain.**

● **How is this experience similar to giving genuine love in real life?**

Ask the Twos:

● **How does it feel to be receiving love from the people on either side of you?**

● **How is this experience like receiving genuine love in real life?**

Say: **Real love is a free gift. It carries no price tags, no punishment, no conditions. That's the kind of love we're going to talk about today.**

■ Love Banners

(20 to 25 minutes)

Supplies: Bibles, heavy aluminum foil, permanent markers, streamers, tape, magazines

Have students form two groups, and have groups gather at opposite corners of the room. Set out heavy aluminum foil, markers, streamers, and tape. Give one group a set of Bibles and magazines such as Family, Child, GROUP Magazine, and CCM Magazine. Give the other group only popular-

Understanding Unconditional Love

In a culture in which the law of give-and-take is the norm, asking people to buy into a love that's unconditional may actually strike them as unhealthy or codependent. They might say unconditional love would be self-destructive or even self-abusive. After all, if you must love people unconditionally, what do you do if they start abusing you? Just forgive them and stay with them?

If students bring up this argument, discuss the biblical distinction between "loving" someone and "having a relationship" with him or her.

The Bible never commands us to participate in any sort of unconditional relationship. That is, we're never told we have to be in relationship with a particular person regardless of his or her behavior. As Christians, there are conditions set on all our relationships—with God (see Matthew 24:13; Mark 16:16; and John 10:9) and with others (see Matthew 18:15-17).

However, we are commanded to *love* others unconditionally. So if a person loves someone who is abusive, he or she doesn't have to stay in relationship with that person—but does have to keep loving that person.

To help people see how they can love others this way, have them consider their lives from God's perspective. He *loves* all the people in the world equally but has a *relationship* with only a relative few.

culture magazines such as People, Sassy, YM, GQ, and Rolling Stone. (Don't give Bibles to the second group.)

Have the Bible group use the supplies you've provided to create a "Real Love" banner that describes love based on these passages: 1 Samuel 20 and 1 Corinthians 13:4-7. Have the other group create a "Worldly Love" banner that describes love based solely on the magazines you've given them.

Ask both groups to use the foil to make their banners; then have groups hang the banners vertically in their assigned corners. Encourage students to decorate the banners by finding or drawing pictures, writing poems or phrases, and using signs or symbols that identify their assigned love.

When groups are finished, have each person find a partner from the other group. Have pairs tell each other about their respective banners. Then have pairs discuss these questions:

● **What stands out to you the most about these two banners?**
● **Which kind of love are you most familiar with? Explain.**
● **Which kind of love are you the most drawn to? Explain.**
● **When have you seen an example of love that always comes with a price tag? of love that's always free?**

Have a volunteer read aloud 1 Corinthians 13:4-7. Then say: **Real love is a free gift. The Bible is full of examples of relationships that illustrate real love—the kind of love found in 1 Corinthians 13:4-7. For example, David and Jonathan shared a special friendship that** was based on real love. They both had the power to manipulate others to get their way, but they chose not to. They turned away from false love and chose the real thing instead.

Understanding the Nature of Love

Ever wondered about the true nature of love? You're not alone. Here's just a smattering of what people through the ages have said about love:

● "Love is ever the beginning of knowledge, as fire is of light."

—Thomas Carlyle

● "Love is the life of man."

—Emanuel Swedenborg

● "Love is the medicine of all moral evil."

—Henry Ward Beecher

● "Love is the hardest lesson in Christianity; but, for that reason, it should be most our care to learn it."

—William Penn

Learning to love unconditionally *is* a hard lesson—especially for people who rarely see real love in action. Thankfully, God's Word reveals a picture of love that's true for all people—a love that never wavers, never changes, and never fails.

In the famous "love chapter," 1 Corinthians 13, Paul uses the Greek word "agape" when describing real love. That word speaks of a love born out of recognizing a person's or object's inherent value. It is a selfless, other-focused love. It is unconditional and rests wholly on the intrinsic value of the one loved, not upon his or her behavior.

As students study this passage, explain to them the meaning of "agape." Then they'll be better able to understand why real love must always be a free gift.

Leader tip ▼

If you have more than twelve students, you can streamline this activity by having students form separate "love" groups of six or more, or by asking more than three volunteers to kneel at one time.

■ Love Without Strings

(20 to 25 minutes)

Supplies: Heavy aluminum foil, tape, permanent markers, cassette or CD player, cassette or CD

Say: **To put all we've learned about real love into action, let's take time now to offer genuine, real love to each other.**

Gather people around the Real Love banner, and have three volunteers kneel in front of it with their backs to the group. Have other volunteers tape a sheet of aluminum foil to the back of each kneeling person. Ask the kneeling students to close their eyes.

Play music in the background—preferably about friendship or God's love. Then ask other students to come behind each kneeling student and use a permanent marker to write on the foil a characteristic of real love they see in that person. For example, someone might write "You always care about people's problems" or "You give without expecting anything in return."

After the first three students have each been "loved" by most of the group, ask three more students to kneel. Begin the process over again, and continue until everyone has been "loved."

Have students remove the foil from their backs and read what others wrote. Then say: **These foil sheets are your personal "Love Banners." I encourage you to keep them to remind you of the love you show others and to remember that real love is a free gift.**

True Friendship Love

Of all the relationships in the Bible, the friendship between David and Jonathan is often looked upon as a model of the pure, godly love all Christians should share with one another.

And no wonder. These two men of God were willing to die for each other—and more.

In 1 Samuel 20, the Hebrew word translated "love" is "ahab" In this passage, the word suggests the importance of not only feeling close to someone but also of treating them with honor, the way God would want them to be treated.

We can learn more about how to have this kind of love in our own lives by looking more closely at David and Jonathan's friendship. Read through the list below, and look for ways you can begin to develop friendships like David and Jonathan shared.

Jonathan comforts David. . . . . .1 Samuel 20:1-2

David is honest with Jonathan, even though what he's saying
may be hard for Jonathan to handle. . . . . .1 Samuel 20:3

Jonathan believes David and is willing to do anything to help him. . . . . .1 Samuel 20:4

Jonathan is willing to risk his own safety to help David. . . . . .1 Samuel 20:5-13

Jonathan is willing to let David become king over Israel, even
though Jonathan is the rightful heir. . . . . .1 Samuel 20:14-16

David makes a lifelong promise to show love to Jonathan
and his descendants. . . . . .1 Samuel 20:17

Jonathan defends David before the king, who tries to kill
Jonathan as a result. . . . . .1 Samuel 20:32-33

Even though Jonathan's life is threatened, he continues to be
more concerned about David than himself. . . . . .1 Samuel 20:34

Jonathan warns David to flee, and they part in tears
because of their love for each other. . . . . .1 Samuel 20:35-42

■ Group Prayer

(up to 5 minutes)

Supplies: None needed

Ask:

● **Based on what we've learned so far, what kind of love do you desire?**

● **What kind of love do you give most often?**

Ask people to choose a place to stand between the two banners according to which kind of love they feel from others most often. For example, if students feel that most people love them conditionally, have them stand closer to the Worldly Love banner. Or if they feel that most people love them unconditionally, have them stand closer to the Real Love banner.

Once they're in position, say: **Look around. It seems a lot of us feel loved—or unloved—in the same ways. Turn to someone near you, and tell that person one reason they're worthy to be loved unconditionally. Then kneel on the floor and pray together for God to teach you the secret of how to give love to others as a free gift.**

Once everyone has finished praying, dismiss the study.

"Love is patient, love is kind. It does not envy, it does not boast, it is not proud. It is not rude, it is not self-seeking, it is not easily angered, it keeps no record of wrongs. Love does not delight in evil but rejoices with the truth. It always protects, always trusts, always hopes, always perseveres."

– I Corinthians 13:4-7

Mentor Me!

Connecting With Spiritual Leaders

BIBLICAL POINT: No human authority is perfect.

BIBLE BASIS: Acts 9:1-19, 26-30; 16; 18:1-4, 18-19; 22:1-3; Galatians 1:11-24;
1 Timothy 1:1-4; and 2 Timothy 3:10-17

TOPIC: Mentors

W hen Jesus recruited his disciples, he didn't require them to take a class. No books to read. No research papers to write.

Jesus simply said, "Follow me."

To learn from Jesus, you had to spend time with him—watching what he did, listening as he told parables to the crowds, noticing when he rose early to pray alone. You asked questions, and you paid attention to the answers.

Eventually Jesus' talk about forgiveness, God, and a new kingdom made sense because you *saw* Jesus' teachings lived out in his actions.

No teacher today is perfect like Jesus, but we still learn some things best by watching other people live them out. You want to grow in your faith? Find Christians who know more about it than you do, and learn from them. No matter where you are in your spiritual journey, you have something to share…and a lot to learn.

It's called mentoring. It's called discipleship. It's called growing.

In this study, students will explore what it means to have and to be a mentor. They'll discover they have at least one skill they can teach others, will recognize the value of seeing life's lessons lived out, and will begin to pursue their own mentoring relationships—all which can help them grow closer to Christ.

Before the study, gather together the following supplies:
● Bibles,
● index cards,
● pencils,
● tape,
● paper,
● newsprint,
● markers,
● masking tape, and
● "Commitment" handouts (p. 137).

mentor me!
● No human authority is perfect.

■ Community Building

(up to 5 minutes)

Supplies: Index cards, pencils, tape

As people arrive, distribute index cards, pencils, and tape. Say: **It's time to see what we can learn from each other. On your card write, "Ask me about..." and then list one thing you can teach or explain to others in thirty seconds—for example, a math principle, words to a poem, the plot of a book or a movie, or a biblical verse. Jot it down, tape your card to your shirt where others can see it, and mingle around to see what things you can teach and learn from others. Your goal is to learn at least three new things. Go!**

When everyone has had time to mingle and trade lessons, say: **We've got some talent in this room! And we've got some things we can teach each other. That's how it is with a lot of things—the best way to learn is to get help from someone who knows more than you do. Today we'll talk about how building a one-on-one relationship with a more mature Christian can help you grow in your relationship with God.**

Before you go on, ask people to tell each of their "teachers" one thing they liked about the way he or she taught.

■ Wanted: A Few Good Mentors

(10 to 15 minutes)

Supplies: Pencils, index cards, newsprint, tape, markers

While people are still sharing, tape a sheet of newsprint to a wall. Use a marker to draw vertical lines down the newsprint, about eighteen inches apart. Make sure you create enough newsprint sections so each person can use one.

Say: **This newsprint sheet is about to become our own newspaper classified section. I want each of you to write a classified ad that you might use to search for the perfect Christian mentor. You can write whatever you like, as long as you think it would attract the kind of mentor you really want.**

To help you decide what kind of mentor you might want in your life, I'll give you some questions to think about. You can create your ad based on your answers.

Write these questions on another sheet of newsprint, and tape it to a wall.

● What do you enjoy most about your Christian faith?
● What do you struggle with most in your relationship with Jesus?
● What do you most enjoy doing with other Christians?

When people finish their ads, have them form trios and explain their ads to their trio members.

Have trios stay together when they finish reading the ads; then distribute a pencil, tape, and three index cards to each person. Say: **As we've** just seen, not everyone wants the same kind of mentor or the same kind of mentoring. That's why there are different kinds of mentoring for different kinds of learners. For example, the Apostle Paul pursued three kinds of mentoring relationships in his life to help him grow in Christ. Let's look at Paul's experience to see how these mentoring relationships look in the real world. As you listen, think about which type of relationship would be most appealing to you.

Say: **In the first category are people you admire, such as biblical personalities or Christians who have proven character. These may be people who you'll never meet—people from the past or present. Paul studied the writings of ancient lawmakers and prophets, and from their lives he learned to be "zealous for God."** (See Acts 22:1-3.)

Have people think silently about these questions:
- **What Christian characteristics do you want to develop?**
- **Who has lived them out?**
- **What can you learn from those people?**

Say: **On your index card, write the names of two people you admire who have Christian characteristics you want in your own life. When you're done, tape the index card to your shirt with the names facing out.**

Say: **In the second category are people you can partner with as you grow together. These people are friends who want to grow in their Christian faith as much as you do. You can go through a Bible study together or pair up for a Christian service project. Through your experiences together, you can take time to talk through what you learn—both about the experience and each other. You'll learn deeply and have someone to hold you accountable in making good decisions. Paul met and studied with a Jewish couple in Corinth, Priscilla and Aquila, and when he left, they went with him.** (See Acts 18:1-4,18-19.)

On your next index card, write the name of one person you'd consider partnering with as you work through a personal study or service project. When you're done, tape your card to your shirt, name facing out.

Then say: **The last category consists of older, more mature Christians you can learn from. Is there someone in your church you admire for his or her spiritual life? That's the kind of person you'd like to spend one-on-one time with, talk with about your life, and ask for advice. Paul poured himself into the life of Timothy, who went on to share with others what Paul taught him.** (See 1 Timothy 1:1-4.)

On the last index card, write the name of two older, more mature Christians you'd like to meet with regularly to talk about your life and faith. When you're done, tape the card to your shirt, names facing out.

When people finish, have them read their cards to their trio members and explain why they chose the people they did. Then have trios discuss these questions:

Leader tip

As you describe each type of mentoring relationship, you may want to write the highlights on newsprint so students can follow along more easily.

● **How does it feel to wear the names you chose so everyone can see them?**

● **How is wearing these names like "wearing" the impact a mentor can have on your life?**

● **How do you want a Christian mentor to impact your life?**

Ask trios to pray over their cards, asking God for courage to follow through in pursuing one or more mentoring relationship.

After the prayer, have students remove their cards and set them aside for later.

Seeking Mentors in Print

ere are some readable biographies of Christian men and women you may want to encourage students to read.

The Savage My Kinsman
by Elisabeth Elliot
(Servant Publications)

Elliot's husband was killed by tribesmen who later converted to Christianity under her mentorship.

When You Can't Come Back
by Dave Dravecky
(Zondervan Publishing)

Former professional baseball player who lost an arm to cancer, Dravecky went on to inspire thousands by living the life of an "overcomer."

Joni
by Joni Eareckson and
Joe Musser
(Zondervan Publishing)

Confined to a wheelchair because of a diving accident, Eareckson has become an accomplished Christian artist, speaker, and spokesperson for people with disabilities.

Tom Landry
by Tom Landry
(Zondervan Publishing)

Former coach of the Dallas Cowboys and outspoken Christian, Landry shares his views of winning, living, and standing for Christ.

The Power of a Promise Kept
by Gregg Lewis
(Focus on the Family
Publishing)

Life stories of men who are faithful to family and faith.

■ Bible Exploration

(10 to 15 minutes)

Supplies: Bibles, masking tape

Have students look back at the classified ads they created. Say: **It would be great to find mentors like these. If there were mentors as good as these, you'd probably only need one for your whole lifetime. But no human authority is perfect, and that means even the best mentors we find won't be everything we want them to be. That's why it might be better to think about mentoring as a lifelong process. Many people will come into your life to help you grow, just as many people will come to you so you can help them grow.**

The Apostle Paul provides a great example of this sort of lifelong mentoring in action. Let's look at several points in his life in which he was either mentoring or being mentored.

Put a line down the center of the room using masking tape. This line will represent Paul's life. Have people form seven teams, making sure each team has a Bible. If you have fewer than seven students, assign multiple passages to some people, and ask them to cover more than one area on the time line.

Assign each group one or more of these passages: Acts 9:1-19; 9:26-30; 16:1-5; 16:13-15, 40; 18:1-4, 18-19; Galatians 1:11-24; and 2 Timothy 3:10-17.

Have each group read its assigned Scriptures, and create a summary statement that describes these two things:

1. what's happening in the passage, and

2. whether Paul's experience involved mentoring someone or being mentored by someone.

After groups create their summary statements, place the groups on the time line according to the order of the Scripture passages above. Starting with the situation in Acts 9:1-19, ask groups to summarize the situation they discovered in the Bible passage and how Paul was either mentoring or being mentored.

After all the groups have shared, say: **Look how many times Paul used mentoring to change a life. In his life he was both mentored and a mentor. Paul was human, and no human authority is perfect; however, he allowed God to use others to shape his life and used his life to shape others.**

Have people return to their trios to discuss these questions:

● **How are you being mentored in life right now?**

● **How are you mentoring others?**

● **Since no human authority is perfect, why would you trust someone to mentor you?**

● **Since no human authority is perfect, why do you think others should allow you to mentor them?**

Say: **Because you know people aren't perfect, it can be hard to trust someone enough to let him or her become your mentor. And** it can be even harder to trust yourself enough to become a mentor for others. To help us overcome this hurdle to mentoring, let's see just how "perfect" we need to be to lead others safely.

■ Mountain Climbing

(15 to 20 minutes)

Supplies: Paper and pencils

Have people form pairs, and give each pair two sheets of paper and two pencils. Explain that in each pair, one person will be the artist and one person will be the mentor. The mentor will find an object in the room for the artist to draw, but the artist may not look at the object. The mentor will verbally describe the object to the artist, who will draw the object based on the mentor's description. Then partners will switch roles.

Have partners decide who'll begin as the mentor and who'll be the artist. Then give students five minutes to find an object and complete the drawing. After five minutes, have partners switch roles. After five minutes, have pairs discuss these questions:

● **Were you a perfect mentor? Why or why not?**
● **What made you valuable as a mentor, even if you werent perfect?**
● **What does this experience teach you about mentoring in real life?**

Say: **As you just experienced, no human authority is perfect. But that's OK! To be a mentor, you don't need to be perfect! Anyone who has received something from God can pass it along to others—so you have something to share with others and something to learn.**

■ Commitment

(5 to 10 minutes)

Supplies: "Commitment" handouts (p. 137), pencils

Have students stay in their pairs. Distribute a "Commitment" handout and a pencil to each person. Say: **Knowing that mentors can help us grow doesn't mean much unless we're willing to ask someone to mentor us. Look at the names you taped to yourself earlier as potential mentors. Use the names on those cards to complete the "Commitment" handout I just gave you. When you're finished, share what you wrote with your partner.**

When students have finished and shared with their partners, say: **You can give your handout to your partner so he or she can ask you about it next week, or you can keep it where you'll see it to remind you of your commitment. Decide now. If your partner gives you the handout, remember to pray for him or her and ask next week if the promise has been kept.**

↓Commitment

h a n d o u t

This is when you must make a decision. If you believe a mentoring relationship could be useful to your Christian growth, place your initials here: _____ .

If you initialed the line above, write the name of one biblical character or Christian you want to read about here: _____ .

Write the names of at least three people you know who could encourage your growth if you talked with them about your life:

_____

_____

_____

In the next seven days, contact all of these people to ask if they will consider mentoring you. Be prepared to define what time and effort you expect from them. Also be prepared for the possibility of hearing "no."

If you will contact these three people in the next seven days, sign here:

_____ .

Reality Bites

Why Life Isn't Perfect

BIBLICAL POINT: Sin poisoned the world.

BIBLE BASIS: Genesis 1:27-31; 3:16-19; Numbers 23:19; Psalm 42:5-6; Jeremiah 29:11-13; John 14:1-4; Romans 8:18-27; 2 Timothy 2:11-13; and James 1:2-4.

TOPIC: Discouragement

introduction

Young adults have been disappointed by shrinking opportunities, a seemingly uncaring society, erratic friends, and shattered families. Without a stable knowledge of the truth, they often find themselves in the throes of discouragement—and seeking hope.

Your students need to know that they have an eternal and unshakable Advocate. More than ever, they must know that God is faithful and good, even when all else seems to disappoint them.

In this study, people will explore the reasons behind discouragement in their lives and make models of creation to examine how sin poisoned the world. Through this exploration, people can discover that discouragement stems from sin's initial entry into the world. They can find positive ways to deal with the disappointments they face and see the hope they can have even in the midst of discouraging circumstances.

Before the study, gather together the following supplies:
- Bibles,
- balloons,
- masking tape,
- markers,
- paper clips,
- one "Pop Goes the World" handout (p. 143) for each person,
- pencils,
- newsprint, and
- index cards.

■ Warm-Up

(10 to 15 minutes)

Supplies: None needed

As people arrive, have them form groups of three. Then say: **For the next few minutes, share with your group the most discouraging thing that has ever happened in your life. Everyone in the group must share a story. If you don't want to share your worst disappointment, share one that you're comfortable telling others. While you share, include how you felt and how you reacted to the discouraging situation.**

reality bites • Sin poisoned the world.

When people appear to be wrapping it up, say: **Many of us have gone through some pretty discouraging circumstances. Anger, embarrassment, and sadness are appropriate responses to disappointment. However, if you felt angry while you were telling your story, you may need to forgive someone who disappointed you. If you felt embarrassed, you may need to forgive yourself. If you felt sad, you may need God to touch your sorrow.**

Have people stay in their groups and take a moment to pray for one another. Encourage students to ask God to show them any disappointment that still needs to be dealt with. If some people say they don't have any discouragement in their lives, encourage them to pray for friends or family members.

■ The Dilemma

(5 to 10 minutes)

Supplies: Bibles

When everyone finishes praying, gather the group together, and ask:

● **Based on what you shared in your trios, what kinds of things make you feel discouraged?**

Ask for volunteers to read Numbers 23:19 and 2 Timothy 2:11-13 aloud. Ask:

● **What do these verses say about God's character?**

Say: **God is steadfast and always does what he says he will do.** Then ask:

● **Since God is so faithful and true, why do we feel let down so often?**

Allow a few minutes of discussion, and then say: **We often blame God for discouragement in our lives. But through this study, we'll discover that discouragement is caused by sin, which has poisoned the world.**

■ Pop Goes the World

(20 to 25 minutes)

Supplies: Bibles, balloons, masking tape, markers, paper clips, "Pop Goes the World" handouts (p. 143), newsprint

Say: **Do this next activity with the people that were in your prayer group. After you get back into that group, have one of your group members come and get one balloon, one strip of masking tape, one paper clip, a few markers, and one handout for each person in your group.**

After each group has the necessary materials, instruct groups to follow the directions on their "Pop Goes the World" handouts.

As groups complete the handouts, write the following questions on newsprint, and tape it to a wall:

Leader tip

To save time, you may want to separate the materials and set them on a table before the study begins.

- How did you feel when your balloon was poked?
- If you had made the most beautiful thing ever created, how would you feel about watching someone ruin it?
- How is the paper clip like sin?
- How is it different?
- According to Genesis 3:16-19, what's the result of Adam and Eve's sin?
- Based on that same passage, what's the ultimate cause of discouragement in our lives?

After students finish the handouts, say: **I'd like you to discuss within your group the questions on the newsprint. Be prepared to share your group's ideas with everyone else when you're finished.**

When groups finish their discussions, gather everyone together and ask:

- **What, ultimately, is the cause of discouragement in our lives?**
- **What does the Bible say about the question, "Since God is faithful and true, why do we get let down so often?"**

After people have shared their answers, say: **God created a world that was perfect. Sin did more than get Adam and Eve kicked out of the Garden of Eden. Sin poisoned everything and everyone in God's perfect world. It is at the root of all the discouragement in our lives.**

When students poke the balloons, some of the balloons may pop and some of them may leak air. If this happens, don't worry. The debriefing questions that follow this activity will work no matter what happens to the balloons.

■ In With the New

(10 to 15 minutes)

Supplies: Bibles, balloons, index cards, markers, newsprint, tape

Say: **Knowing why we get discouraged isn't enough. We still need to figure out how to handle discouragement.** Ask:

- **Based on your experience, what's the best way to deal with discouragement?**

Once several people have responded, distribute index cards, and say: **We're going to take some time to look at the directions God gives us for dealing with discouragement. On the index card I've given you, write the following verses: Psalm 42:5-6; Jeremiah 29:11-13; John 14:1-4; and James 1:2-4.**

Take a minute to read each passage and discover what God says about dealing with discouragement. On your index card, write your discoveries.

While students work, write these questions on newsprint, and tape it to a wall:

- Why do you think this passage instructs us to hope in God's redemption?
- How does hoping in God help you deal with discouragement?

When everyone finishes, have him or her turn to a partner to read Romans 8:18-27. Then have pairs discuss the questions you listed on newsprint.

As pairs wrap up their discussions, give each person a new balloon. Say: **Take the index card with the verses about dealing with discouragement, and put it inside the balloon I just gave you. After you get it**

inside the balloon, blow up the balloon, then tie it off.

While the students follow your instructions, set markers in the middle of the room. Say: **Using the markers in front of you, describe what the world will be like when Jesus returns and we no longer have reasons for discouragement. Use words or phrases such as "peace" or "no more hunger" to demonstrate the difference.**

When the people finish, say: **Take your balloon home with you. If you feel discouraged in the next week, pop the balloon, and look at the passages you've written. If the balloon deflates before you need to pop it, take out the card and read the passages. Then thank God for bringing you through the week without discouragement. Thank him for giving us hope in a fallen world.**

Biblical Background

You get what you deserve...
We've all heard the phrase. We all know what it means. But is it true?
Not according to the Bible.

Sometimes our sin leads directly to being discouraged. But the Bible clearly states that many of our personal disappointments have little or nothing to do with our actions. They're a result of living in a fallen world. In John 9:1-3, Jesus tells his followers that it was neither the blind man's sin nor his parents' sin that caused him to be blind at birth. In fact, God had a purpose for the man's ailment. God used it to bring glory to himself.

Some students may think that discouraging circumstances are punishments for sin in their own lives. Help them realize that all people experience suffering and disappointment—simply because we all live in a sin-poisoned world.

Understanding Discouragement

For many people, discouragement is real and immediate. They may not understand how Christ's return has anything to do with their present circumstances. As you explain the verses of hope found in this study, encourage people with the truth that discouragement has as much to do with how we look at disappointment as it has to do with the disappointment itself. Help them see that God doesn't offer life without disappointment, but he does offer life with a different perspective—a perspective that enables us to see immediate circumstances from an eternal viewpoint.

Pop Goes the World
handout

1. Blow up your balloon, and tie it off.

2. Put the strip of masking tape on the balloon anywhere except on the knot.

3. Using the markers and your balloon, create a model of what a perfect world would look like from space.

4. Read Genesis 1:27-31. How is the model you made like God's creation? How is it different?

5. Genesis 1:27 says that God created us in his image. Tell the person on your left one way that you see God's image in him or her.

6. Within your group, pass your model to the person on your left.

7. Straighten out the paper clip, and poke one end through the masking tape on the model you're holding.

8. Pull out the paper clip, and observe what happens.

9. Read Genesis 3:16-19.

Indexes

Scriptural Index

Topical Index